ZEN COLORING BOOK

101 Animals

Kami Moon

Magic Of Coloring

Once upon a time in a color filled world, there lived a boy named Kiyan. He loved exploring the wonders of his imagination and expressing himself by creating art.

One beautiful morning, the sun was shining bright and birds were singing symphonies. Kiyan sat under a tall, old, Oak tree. Suddenly, a butterfly appeared. The sun reflected off of the majestic creature like a light to a mirror. Then, the butterfly landed gently on Kiyan's shoulder. Once again it lifted off his shoulder and started flying towards a group of trees close to Kiyan.

Curiosity twinkled in Kiyan's eyes as he followed the butterfly. When he caught up to the butterfly, he saw a sparkle of light behind a few tall bushes. He put both of his hands in the center of the bush and spread the leaves as a mesmerizing light filled with unthinkable colors seared his eyes. His smile went from cheek to cheek, as he put one foot into the bush at a time. Finally, he was completely emerged in the new universe; as he looked around, he couldn't believe his eyes.

The butterfly led the way as Kiyan followed, on a golden path. Plants and animals filled the vision to his left and right. He saw golden brown lions, birds with unthinkable shades of purple, he saw endless rivers flowing with mellow clear blue, and trees with leaves as green and orange as the eye could recognize.

He began to realize the world around him was made up of all the art and drawings that he had made throughout his life. The lion, with his grandmother. The birds, with his father. And the trees, with his mother.

The boy wished that he could share the gift of how he felt with everyone in the world. So, when he arrived back to his home, he began compiling everything he remembered seeing. After some time, it was eventually complete, his magical coloring book.

Word of Kiyan's magical coloring book spread far, inspiring children and adults alike. People from all walks of life discovered the therapeutic power of coloring, finding peace, happiness, and a sense of calm within its pages. They experienced the magic of creating something beautiful, one stroke of brush, one color and one page at a time.

Remember, each stroke of color you add is a brushstroke on the canvas of your own story. Embrace the magic, let your creativity soar, and watch as the world around you transforms into a masterpiece of your own making. In this transformative coloring book, we invite you to embark on a journey of relaxation, focus, and self-discovery.

Created with the intention of providing respite from the chaos of everyday life, these 101 carefully curated coloring pages are designed to possibly help you find tranquility, ease anxiety, and embrace a state of mindful awareness. In today's fast-paced world, it can be challenging to find moments of stillness and clarity.

That's why we've crafted this collection with the aim of creating a haven of calm within the pages of this book. Whether you're seeking solace from the demands of work or simply looking for a therapeutic outlet to relax and recharge, this book is for you.

Engaging in the act of coloring could promote mindfulness, enhance focus, and foster a sense of inner peace. It is our hope that this book will serve as a trusted companion on your path to personal growth and well-being.

As you immerse yourself in this artistic sanctuary, you will discover a diverse array of patterns, mandalas, nature scenes, and intricate designs that will captivate your imagination and transport you to a world of serenity. Allow yourself to let go of worries and stress as you bring these images to life with your own personal touch. Embrace the therapeutic power of color and watch as your creations reflect not only your artistic expression but also your inner calm and harmony.

We encourage you to embark on this coloring journey with an open mind and heart, embracing the present moment and allowing your inner artist to emerge. There are no rules or limitations here, simply let your intuition guide you as you choose colors and explore various techniques. Remember, the goal is not perfection, but rather the process of finding peace within the strokes of your coloring tool.

And so, dear reader, as you hold this coloring book in your hands, let Kiyan's story ignite a spark of inspiration within you. Let your imagination take flight, and may these pages become a sanctuary where you can express yourself freely. Find solace in the colors, and let them guide you on a journey of self-discovery, creativity, and joy.

Welcome to this enchanting world of colors.

Let the adventure begin!

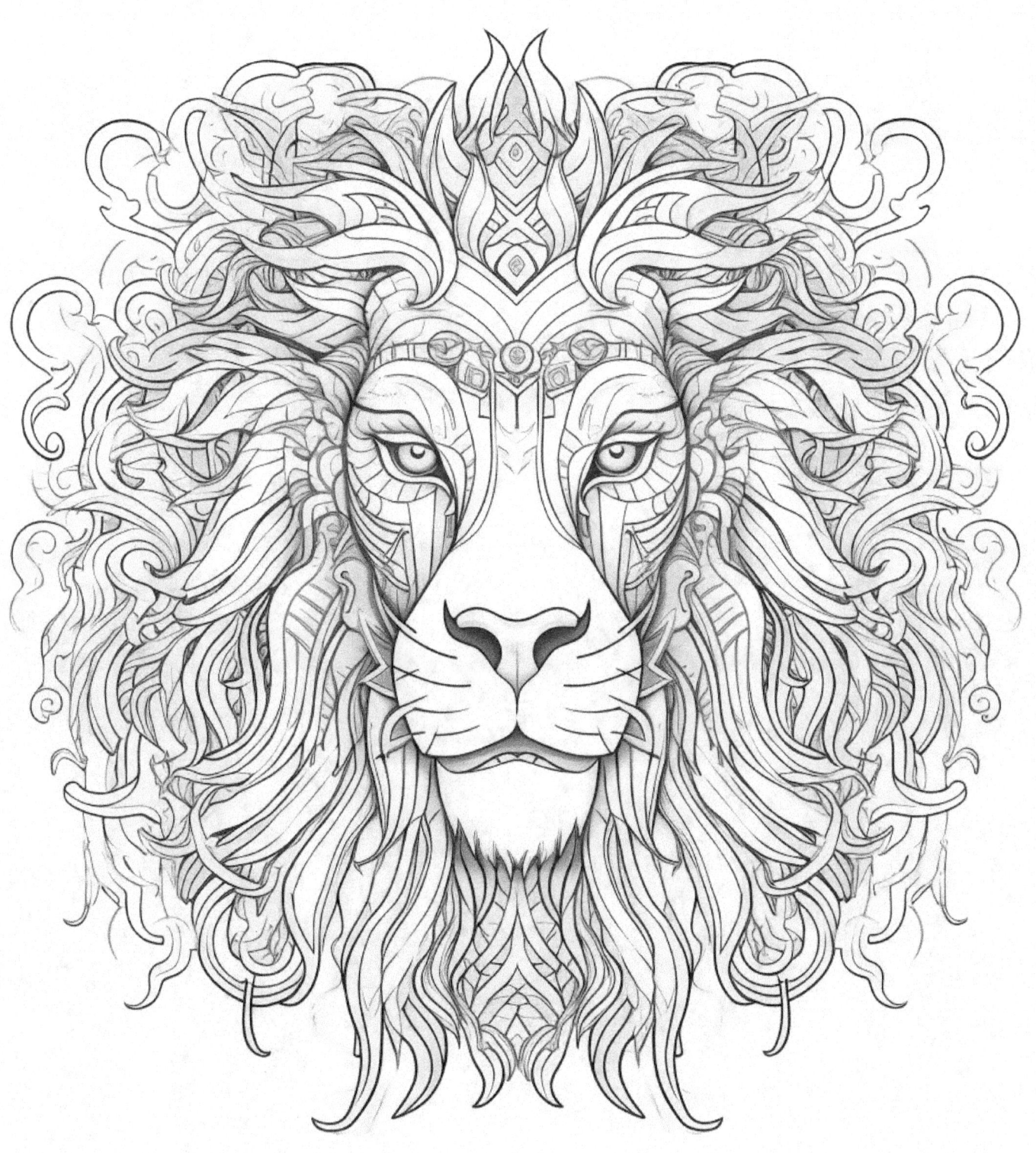

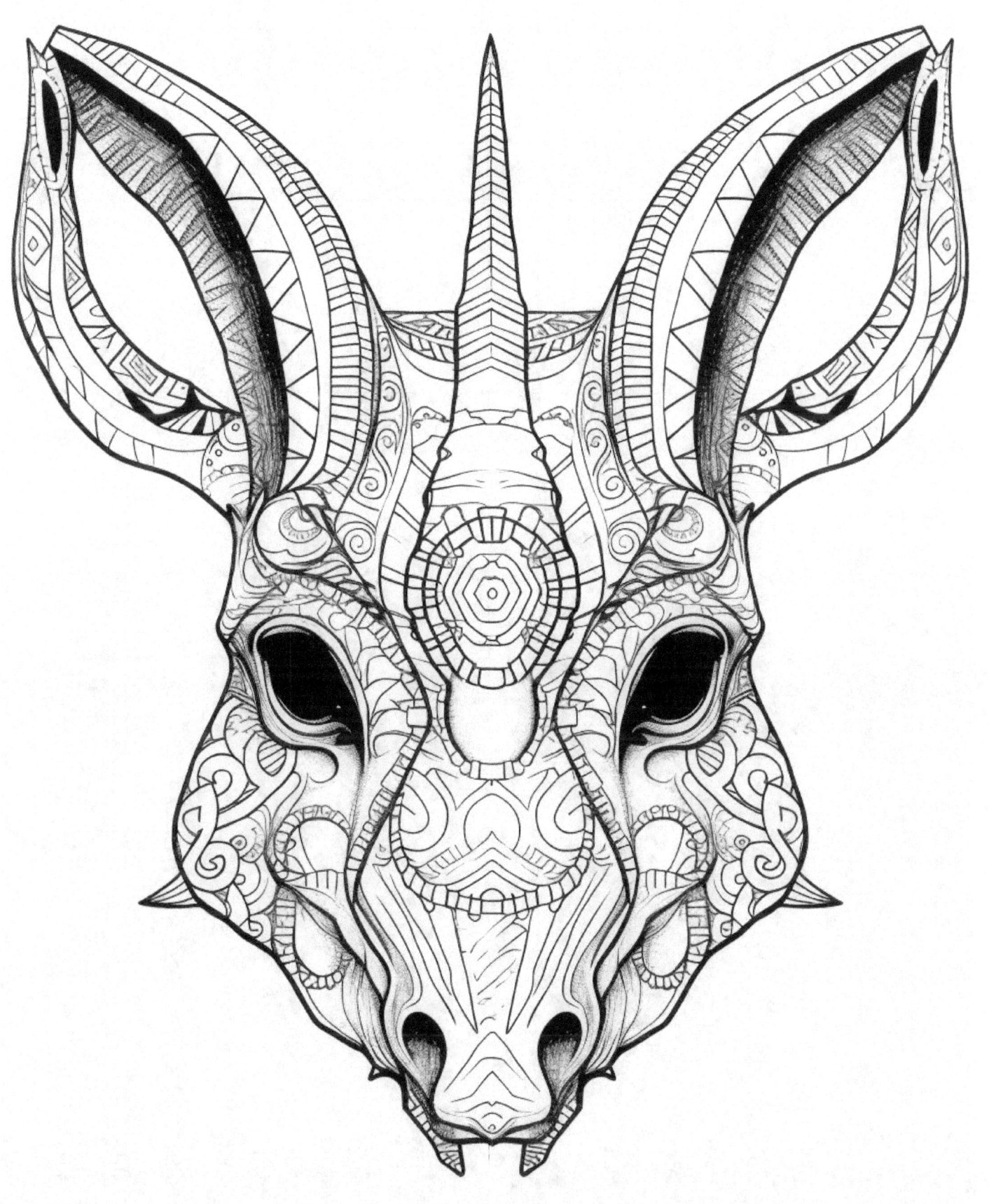

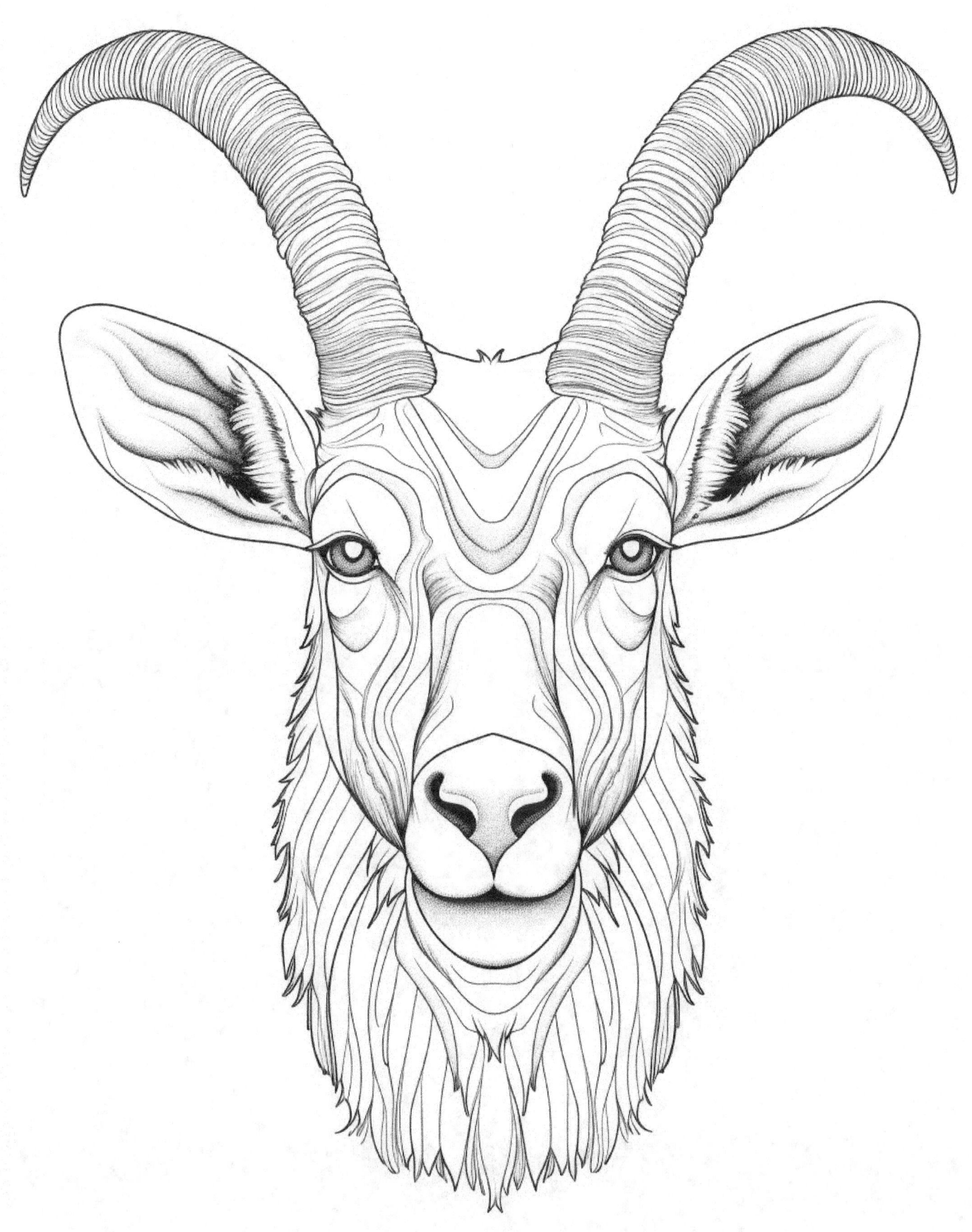

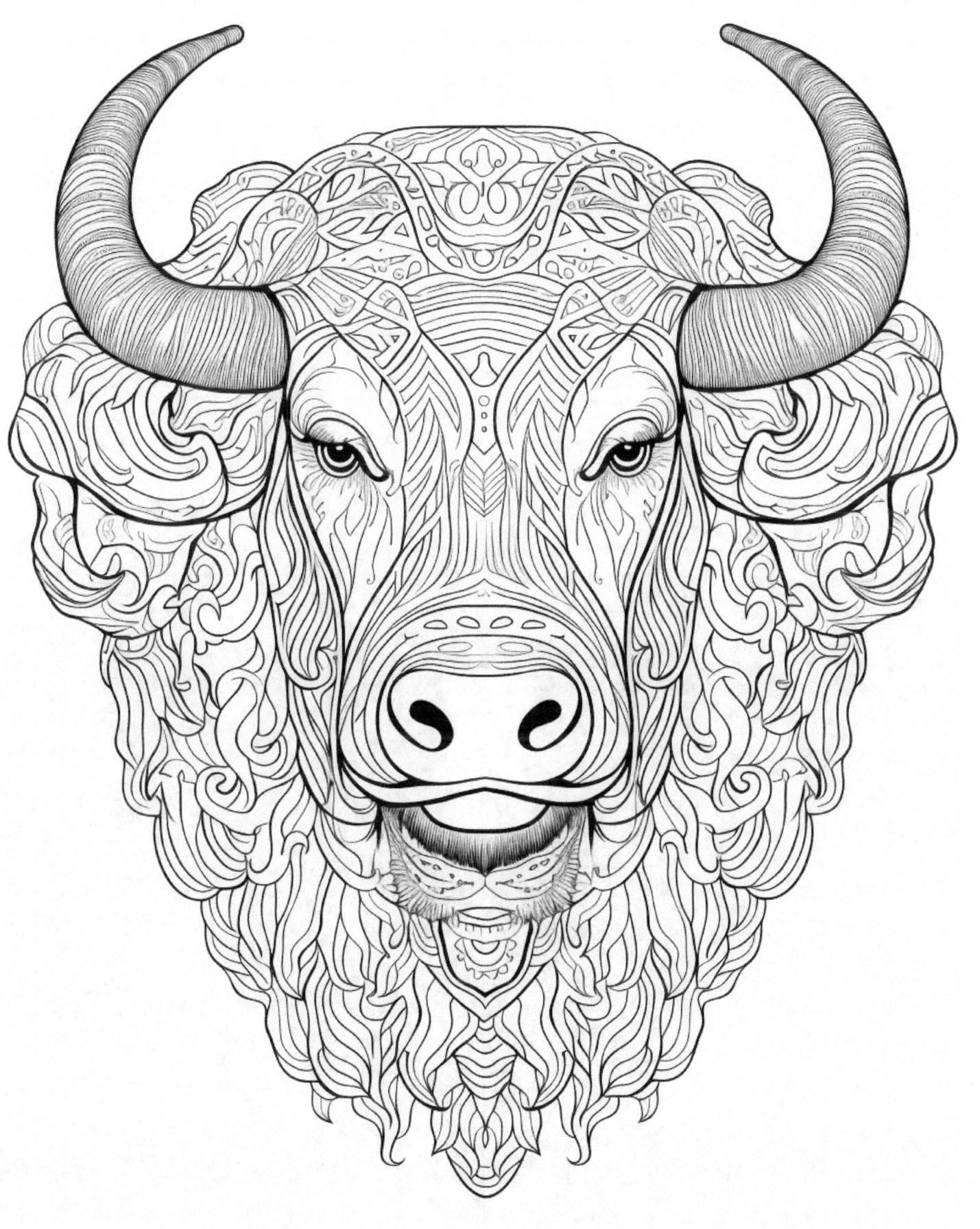

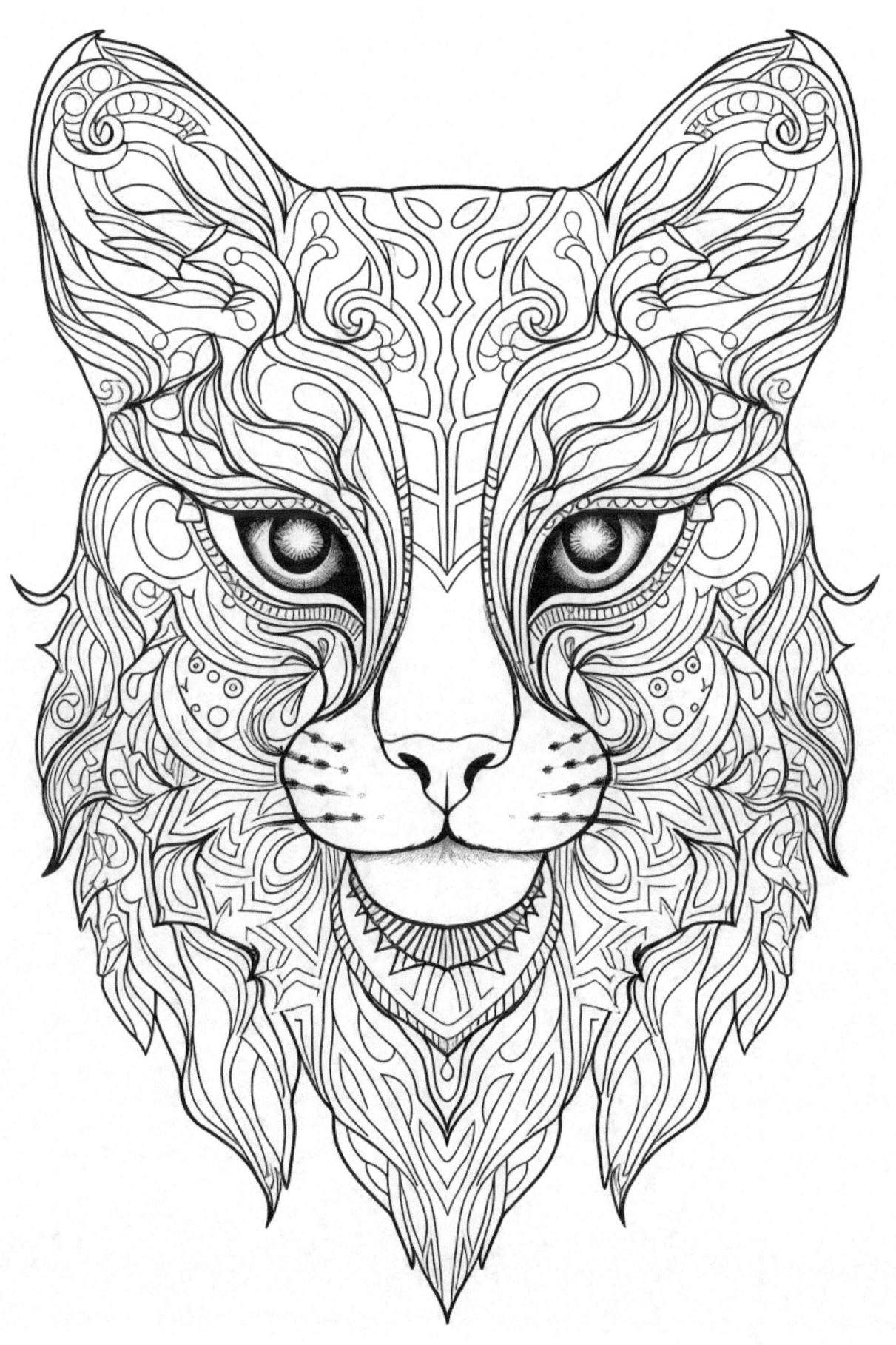

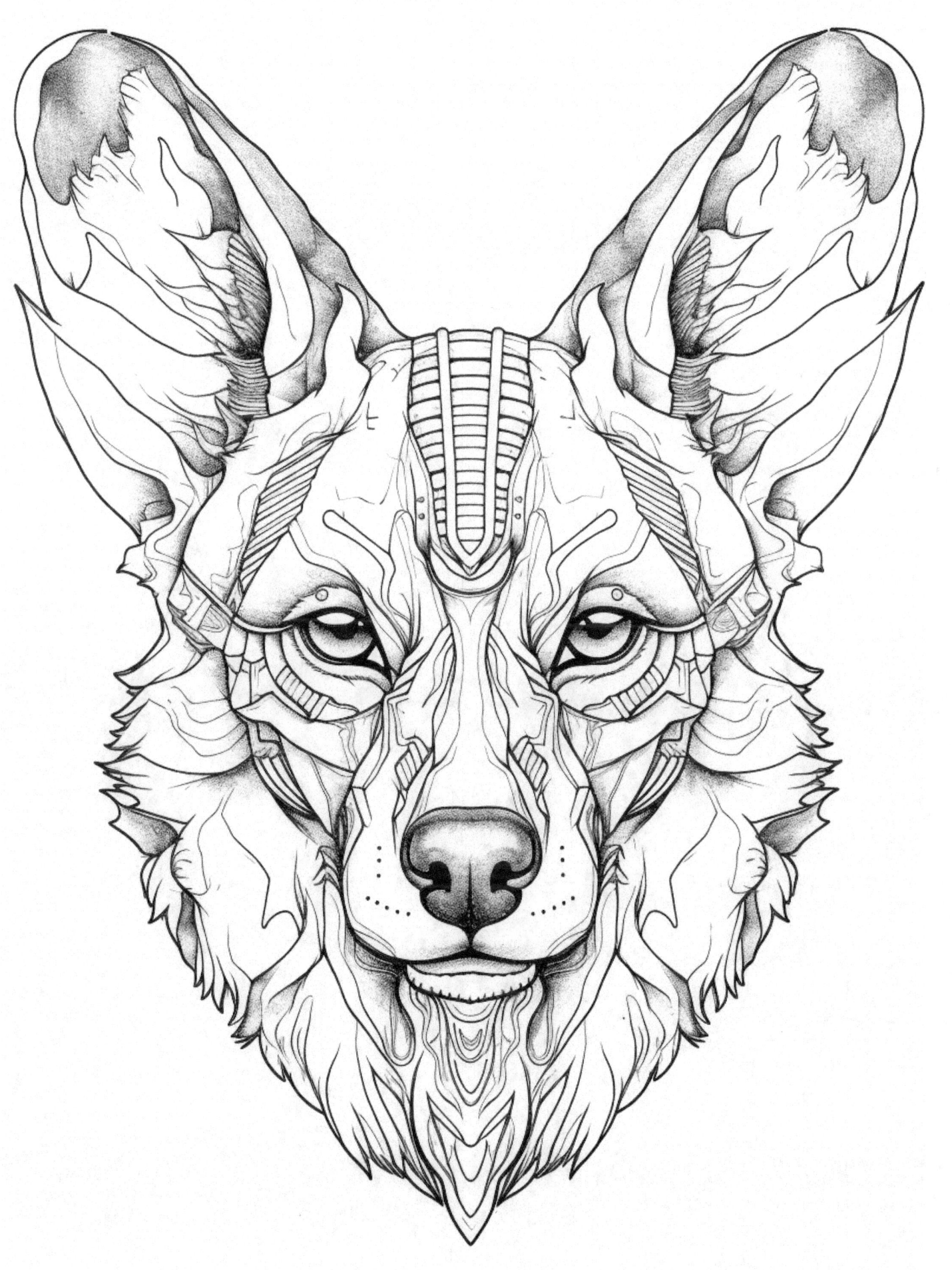

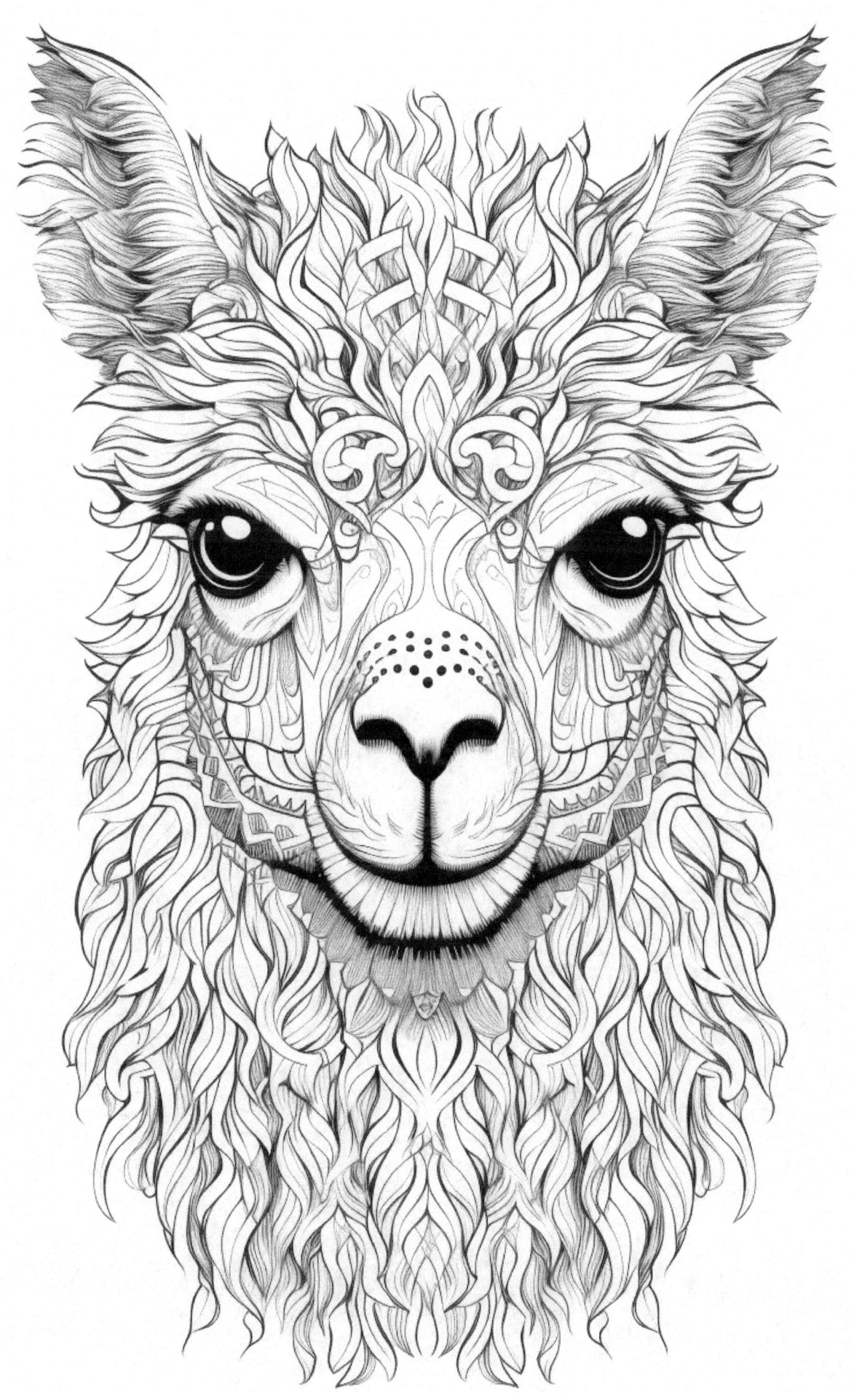

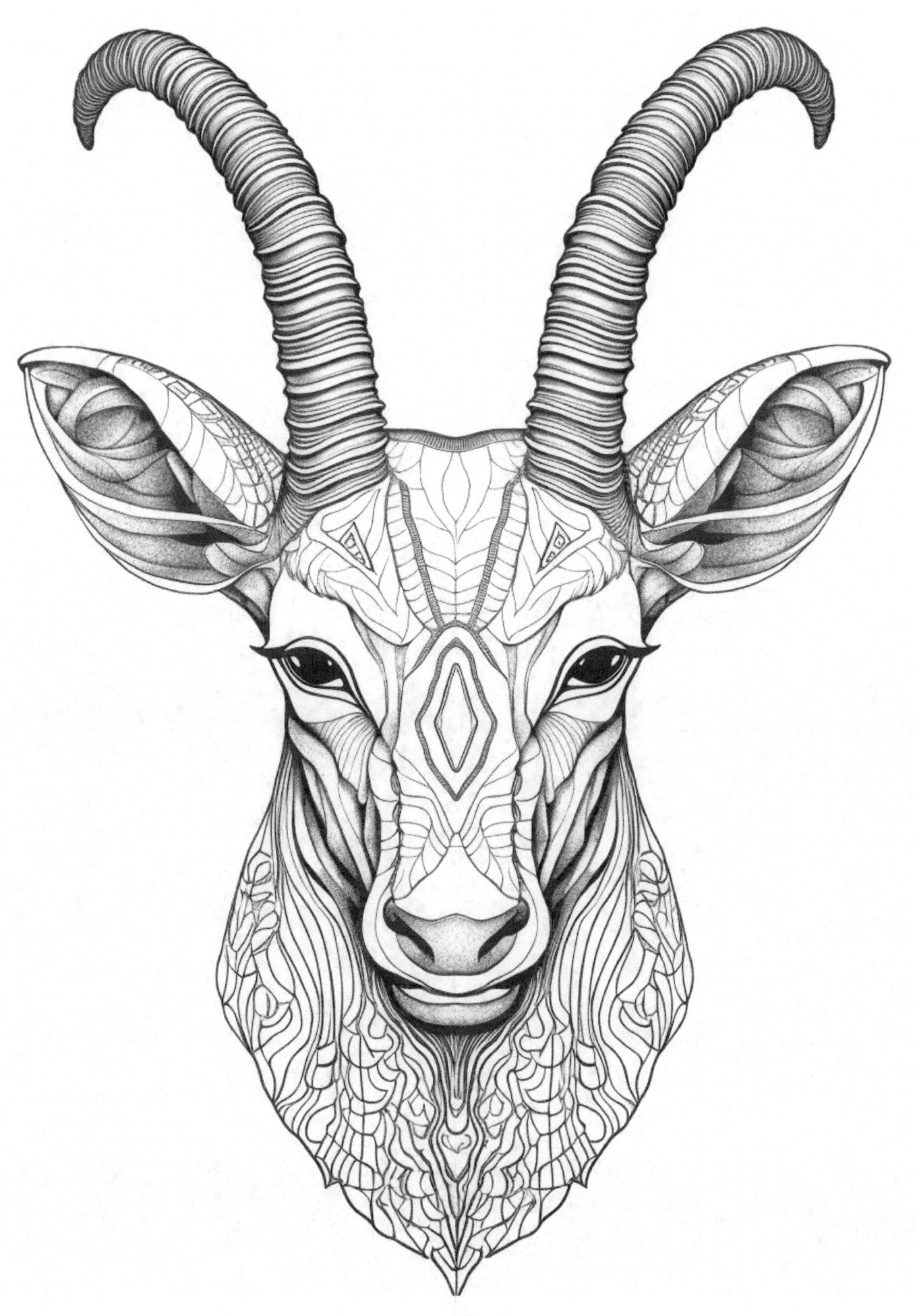

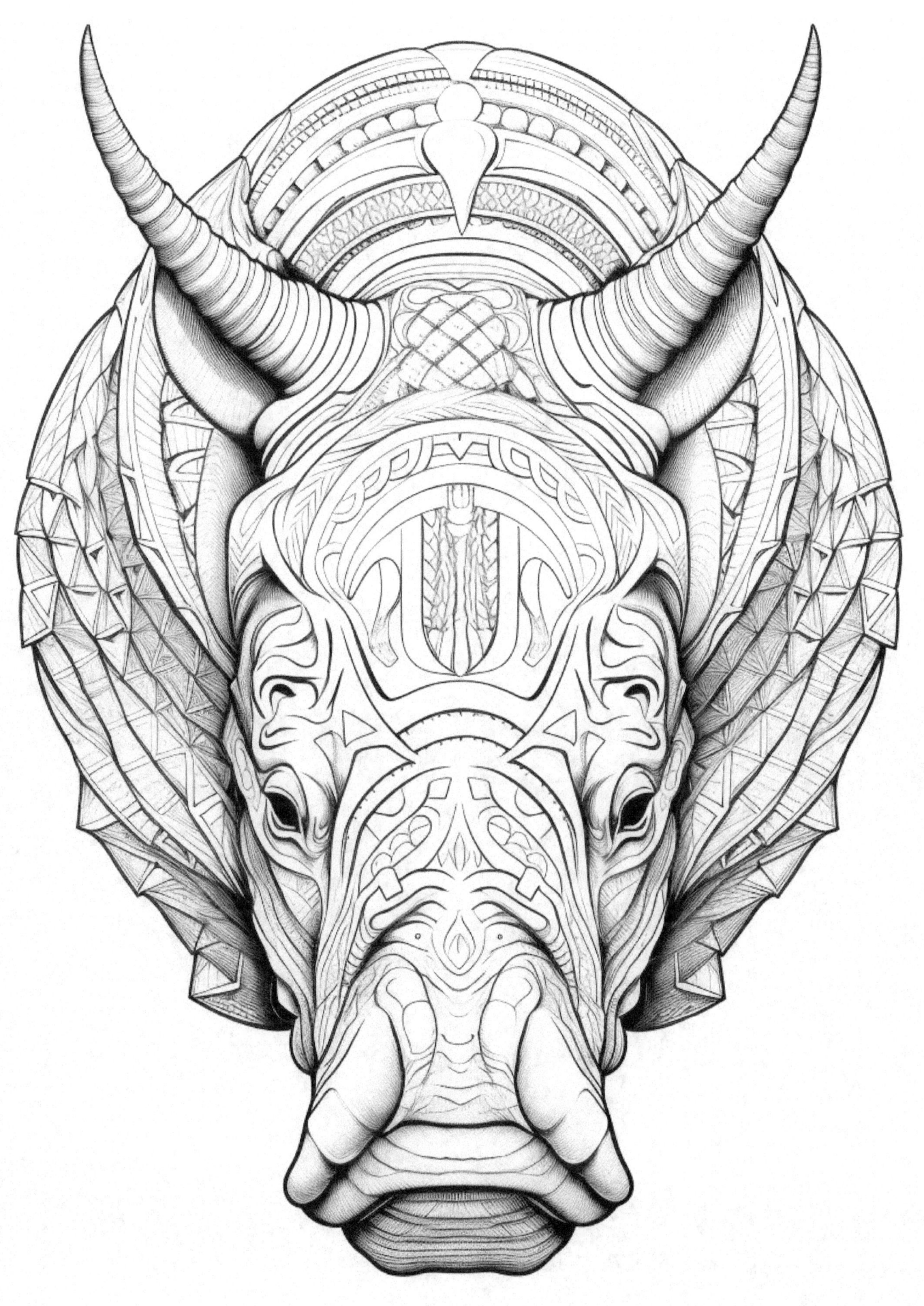

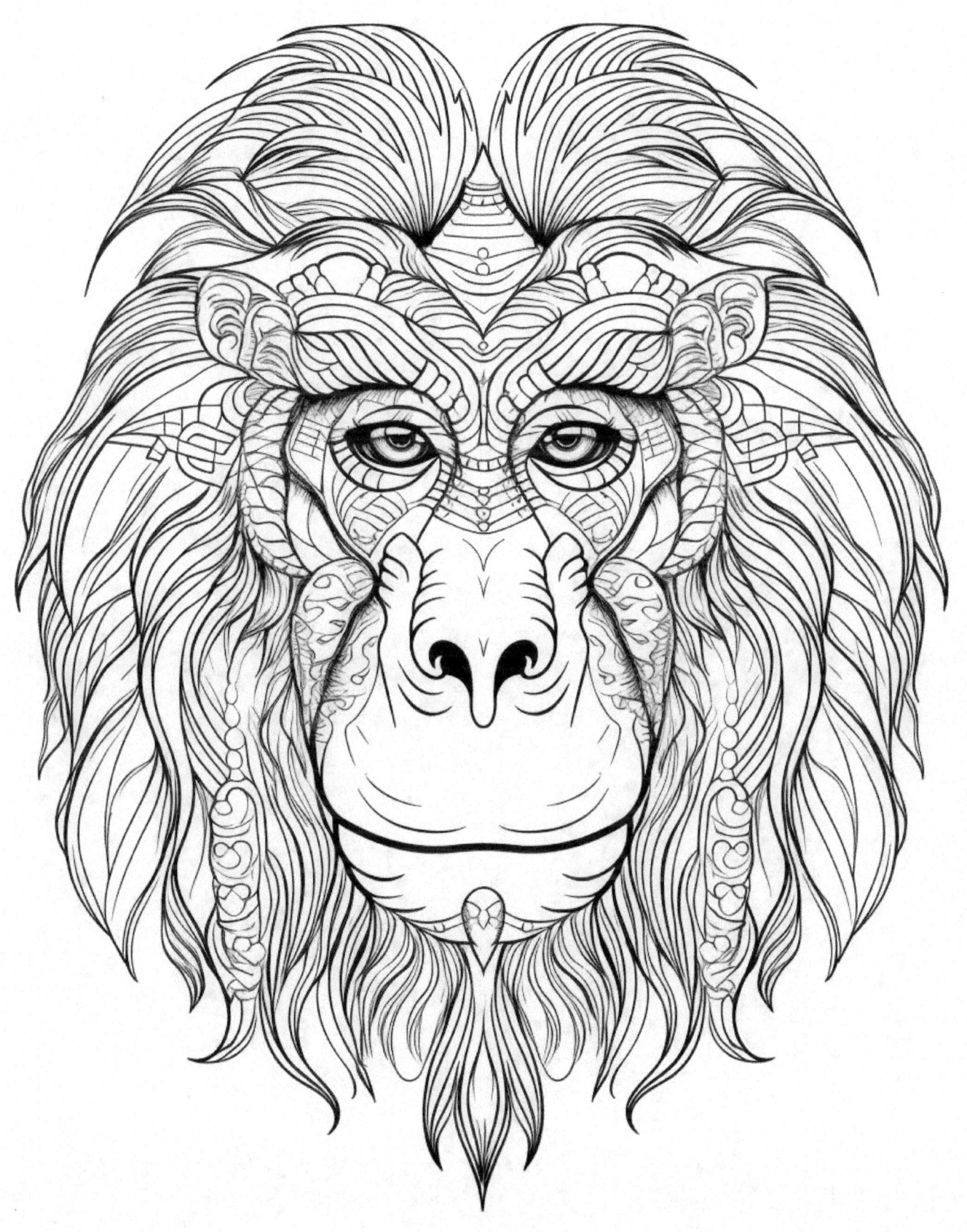

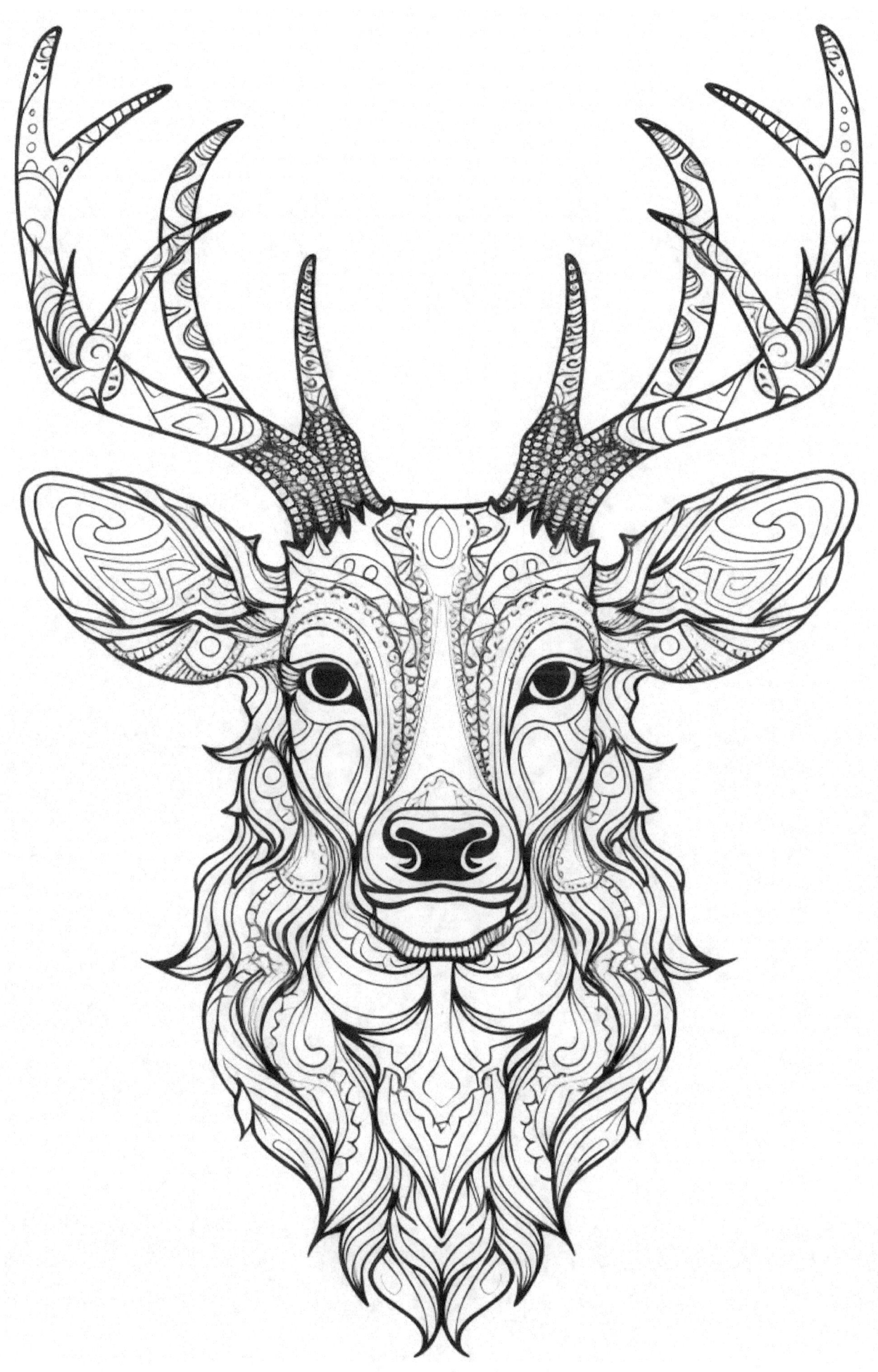

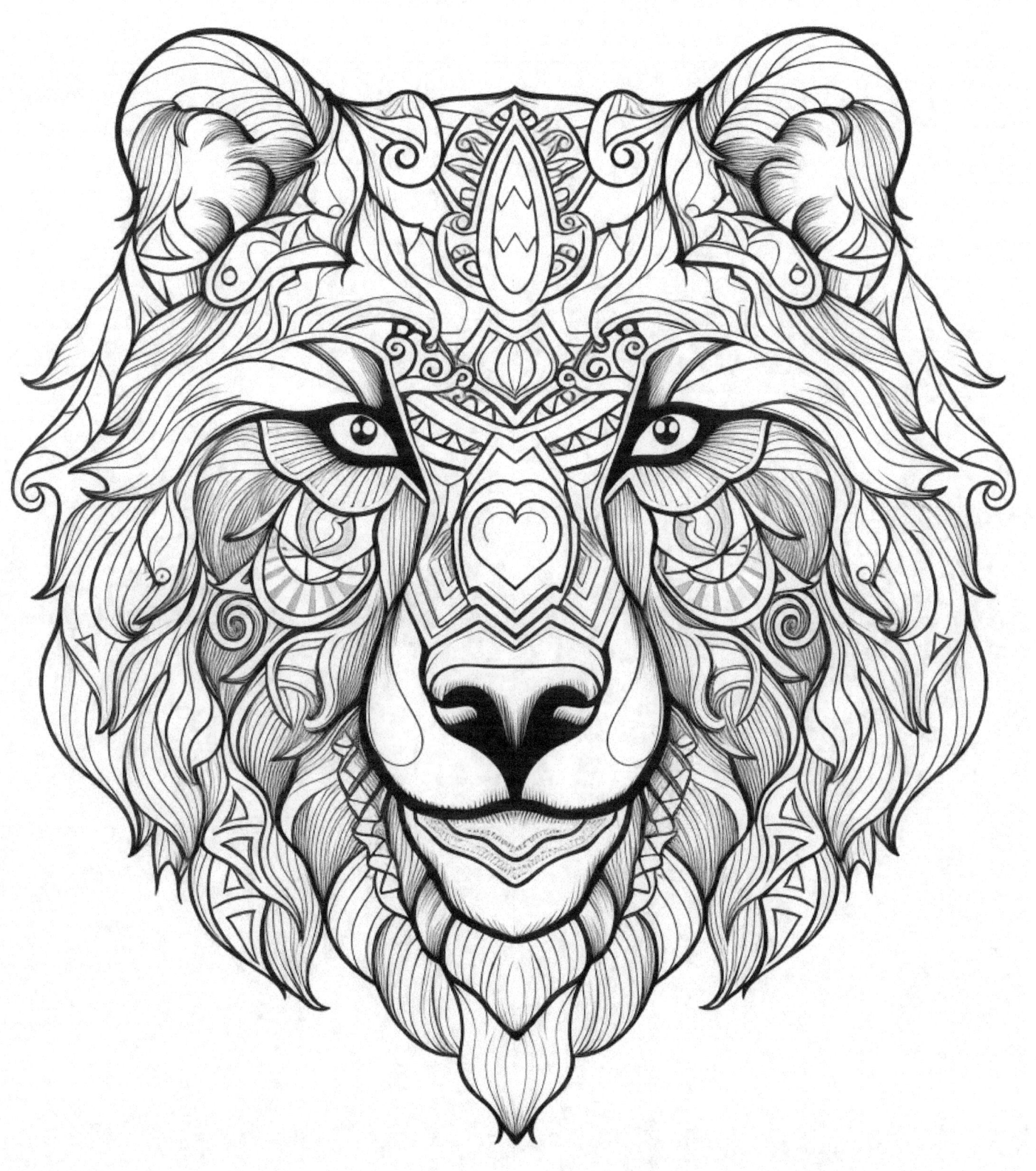

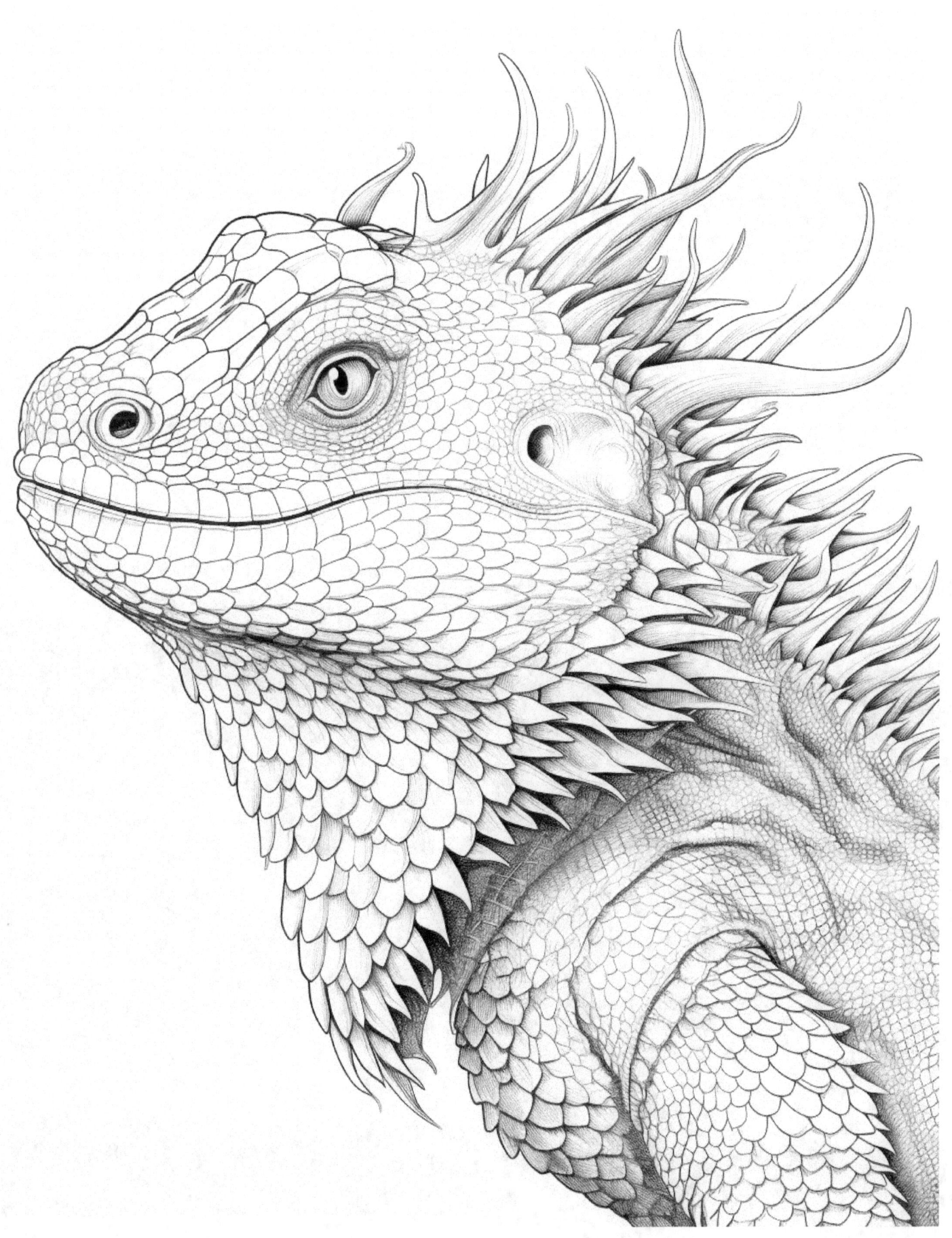

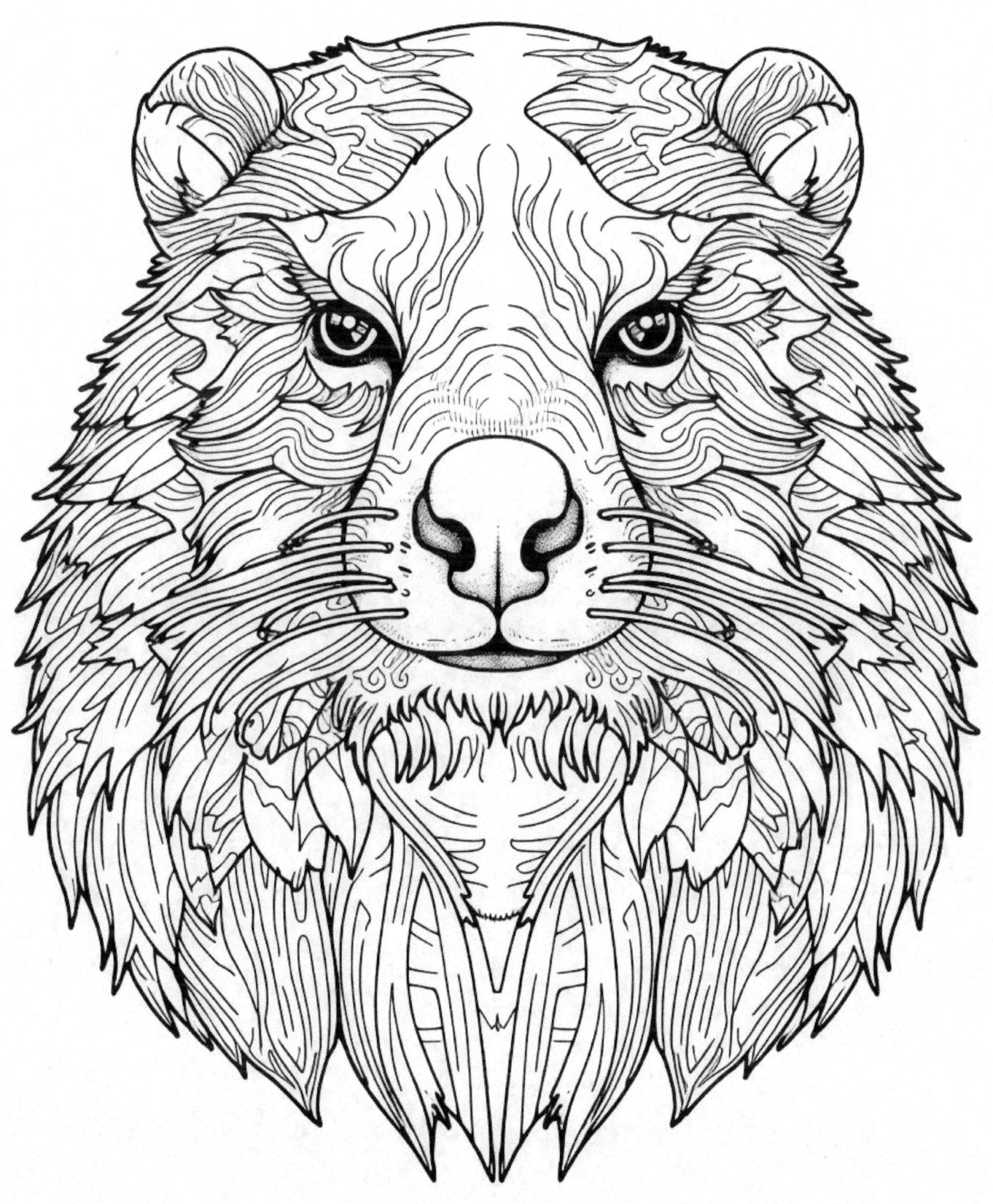

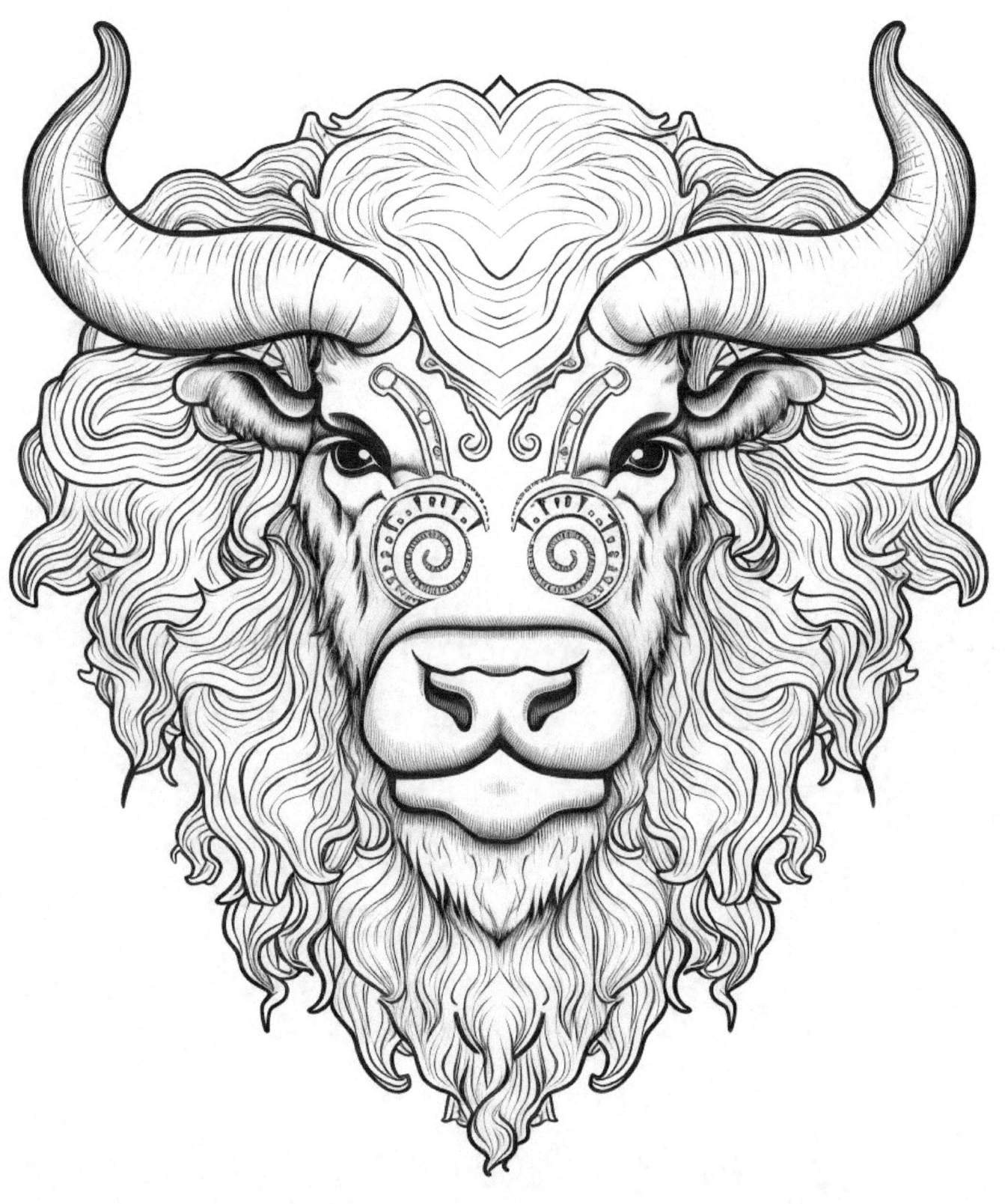

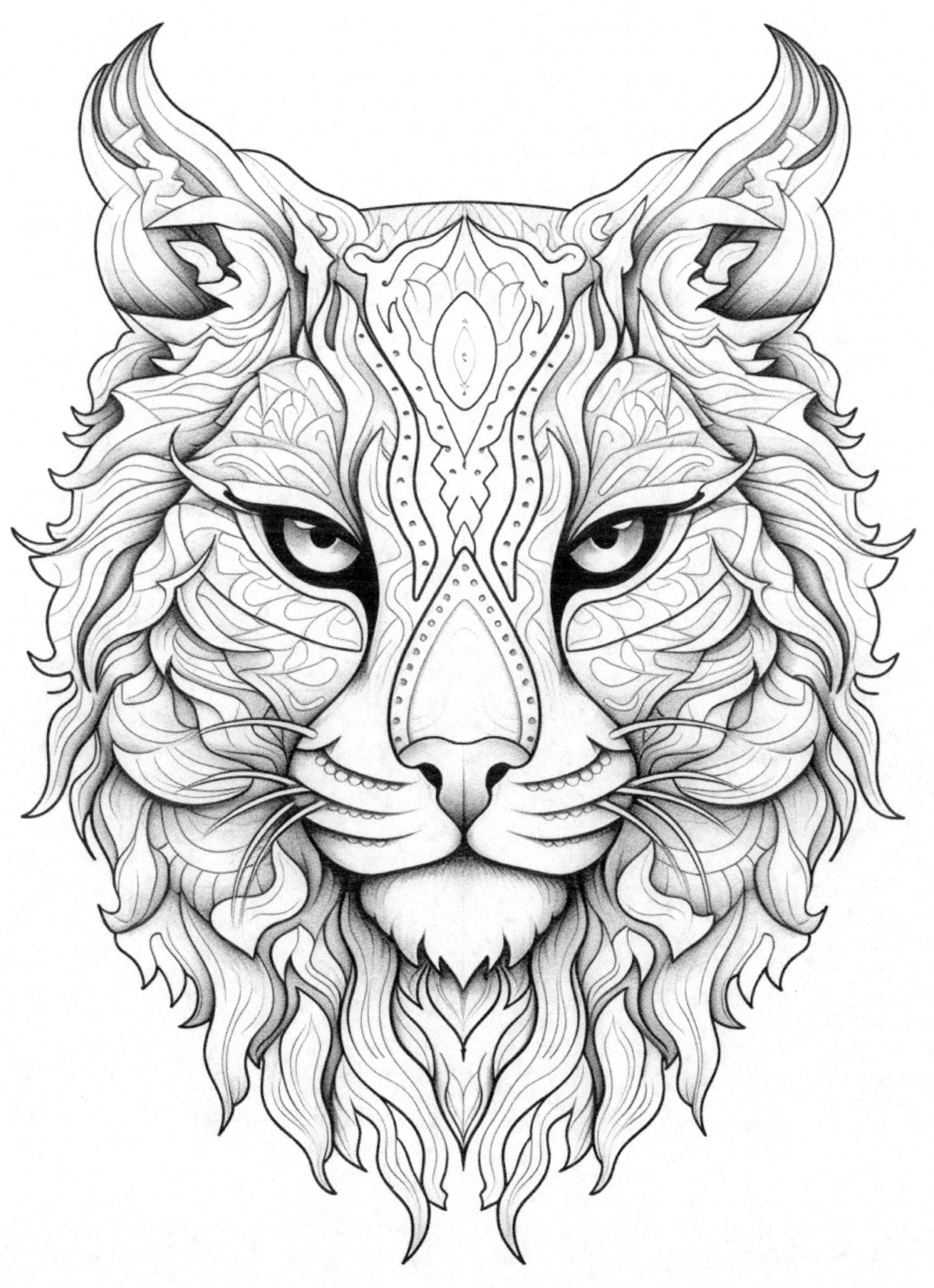

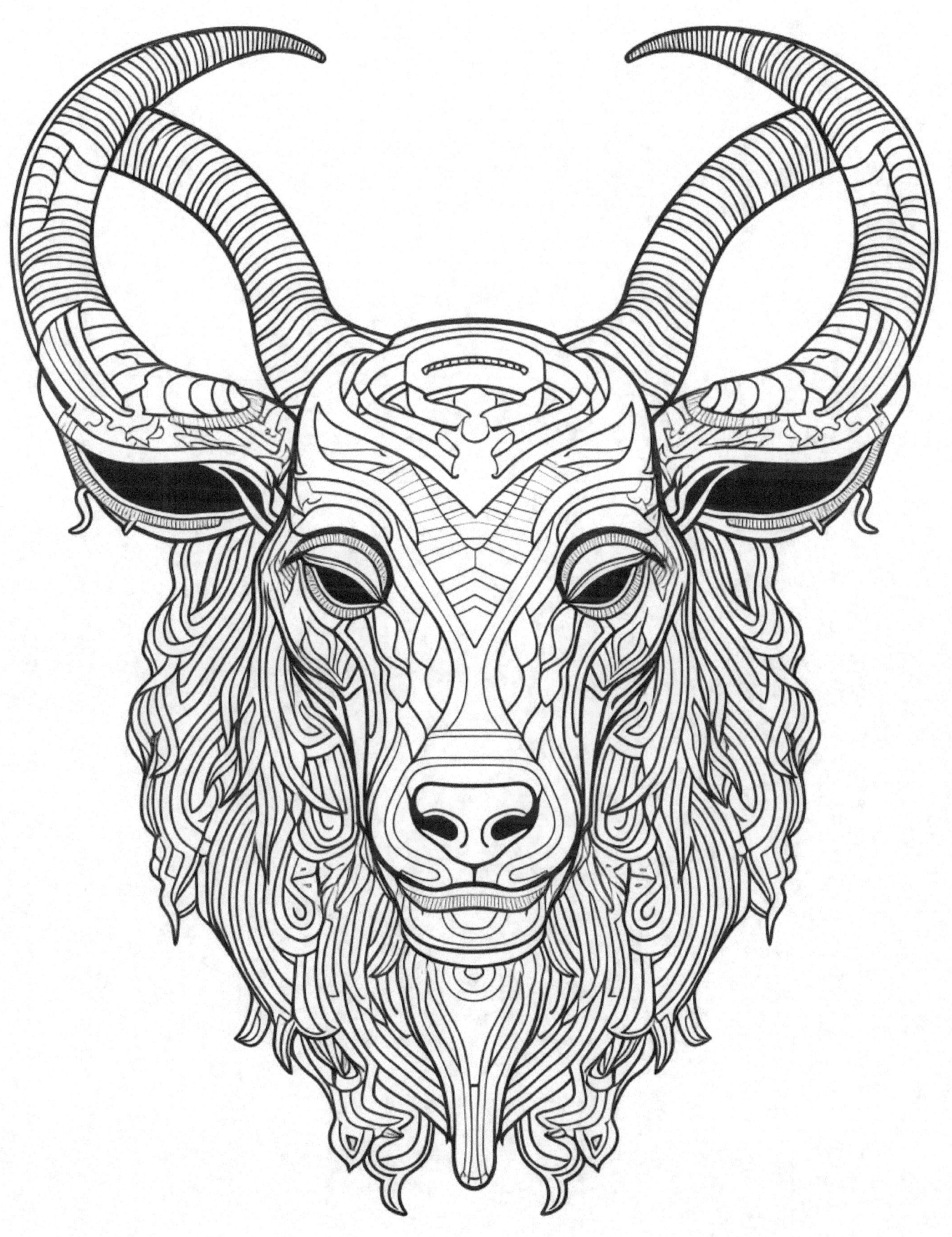

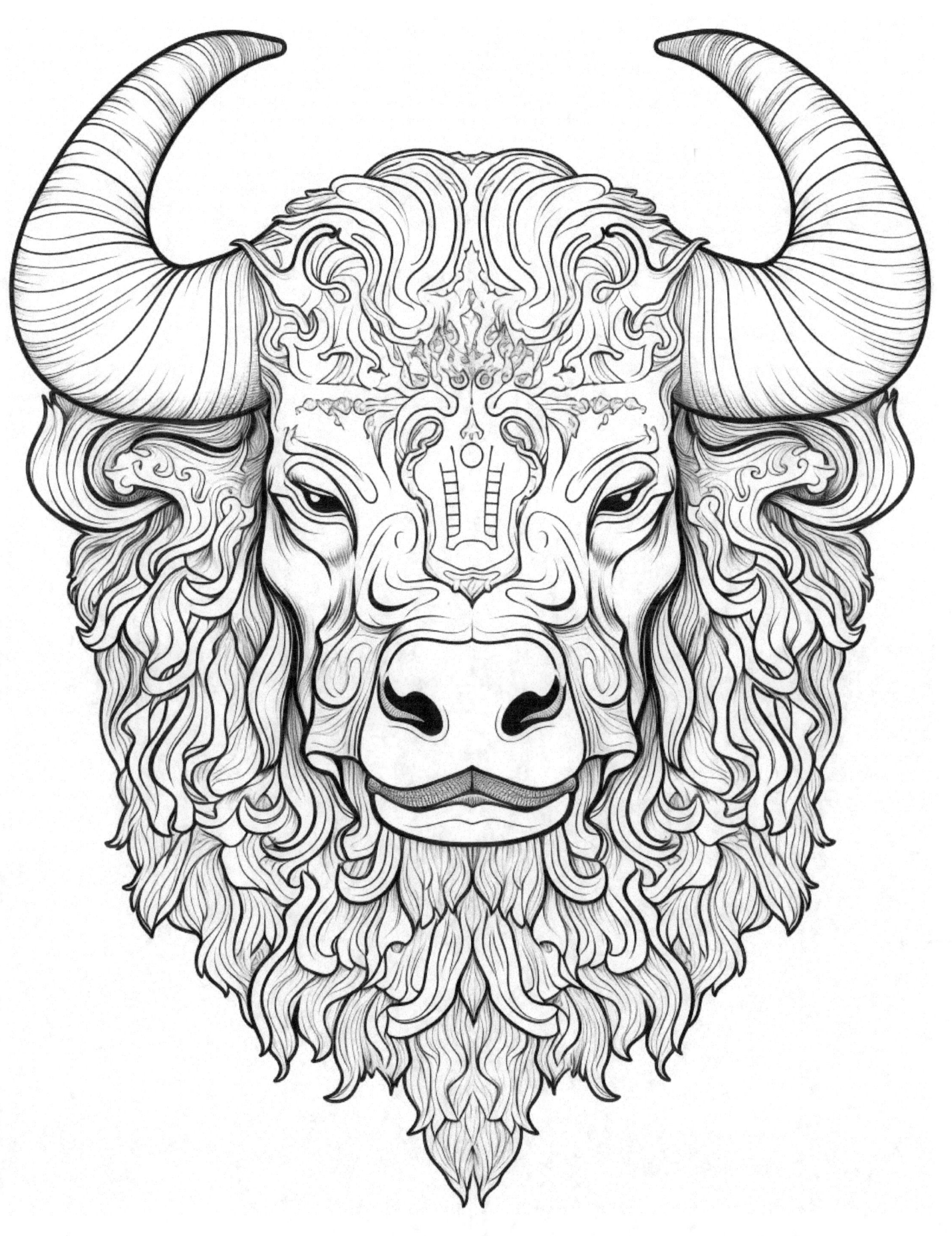

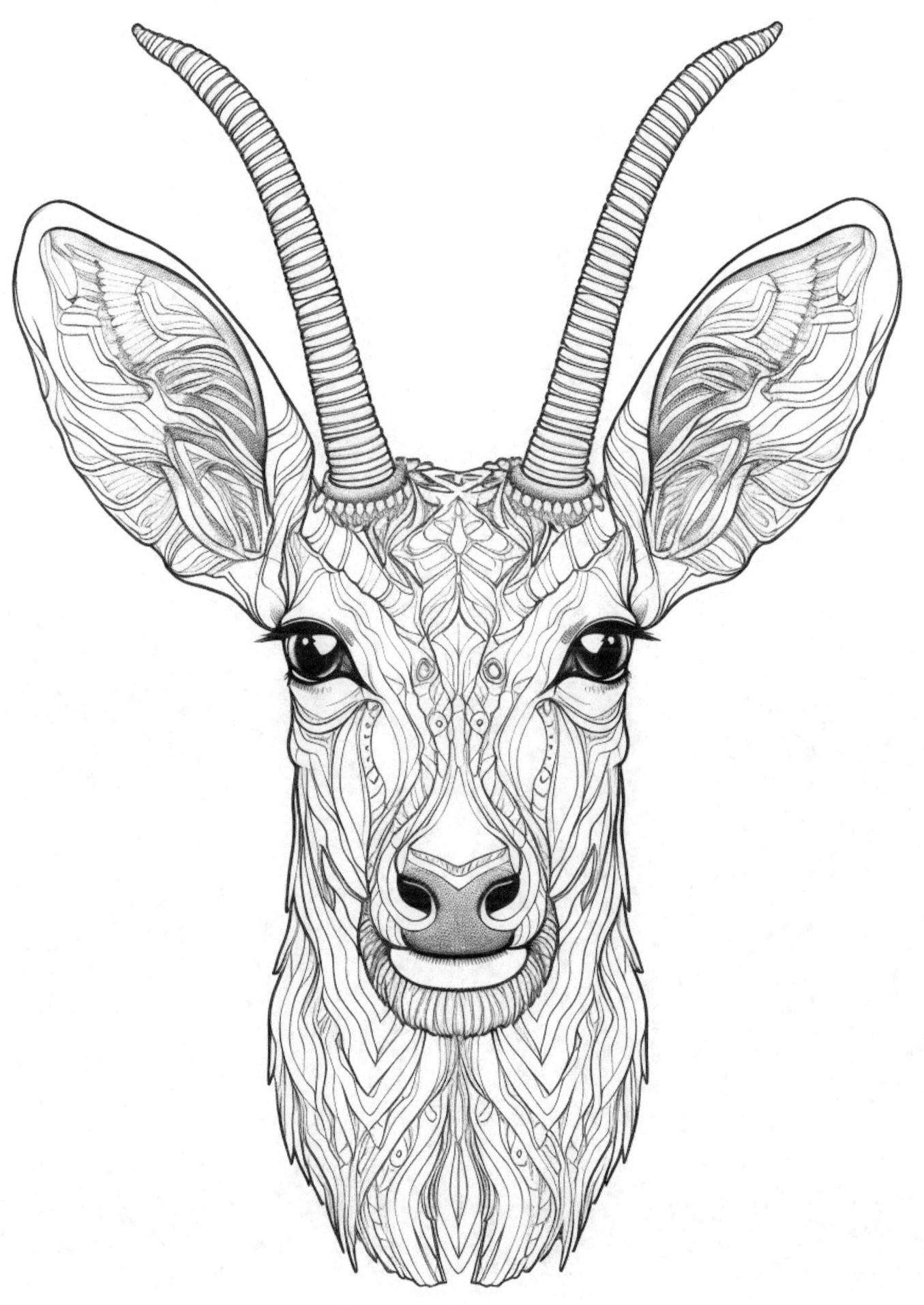

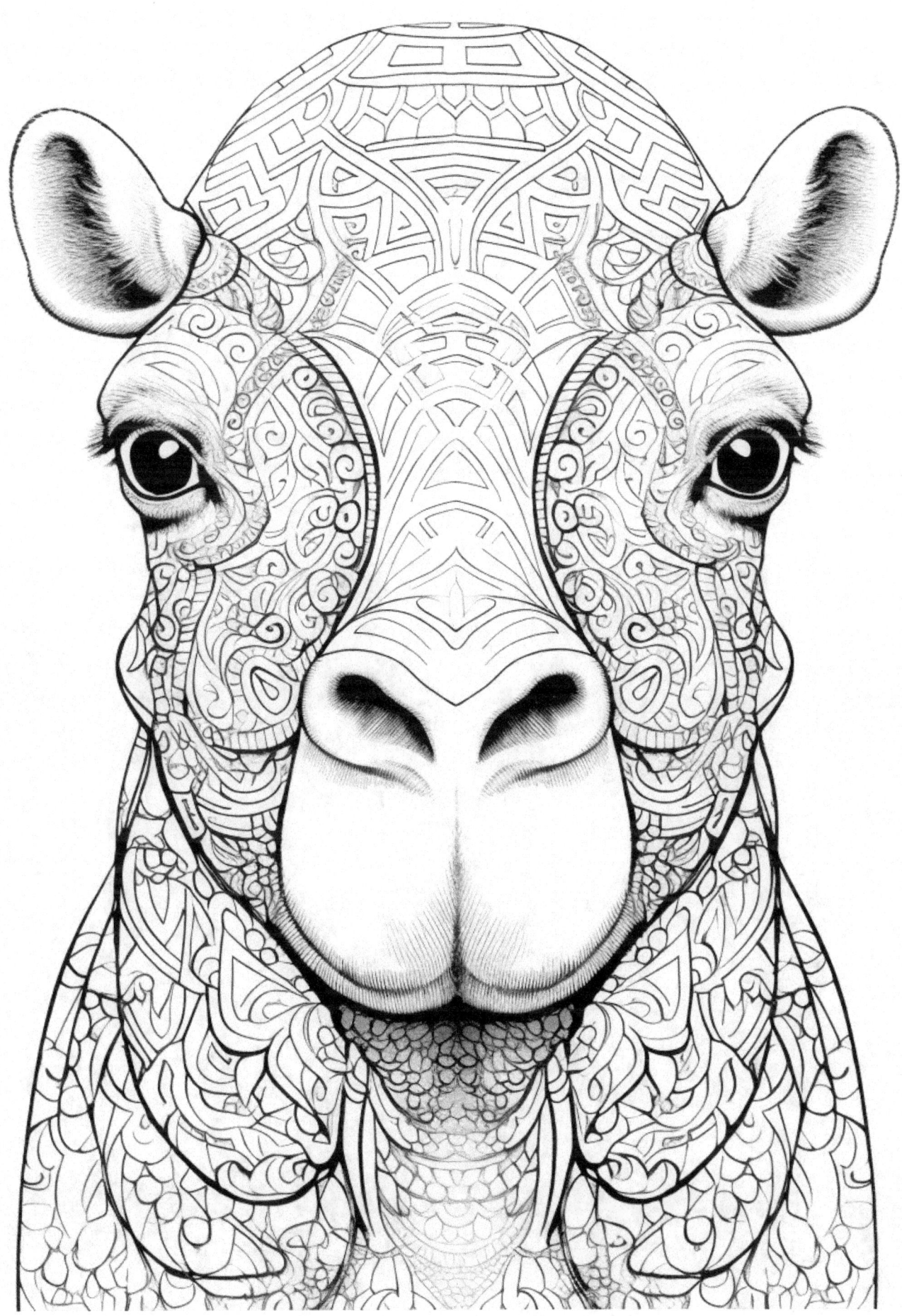

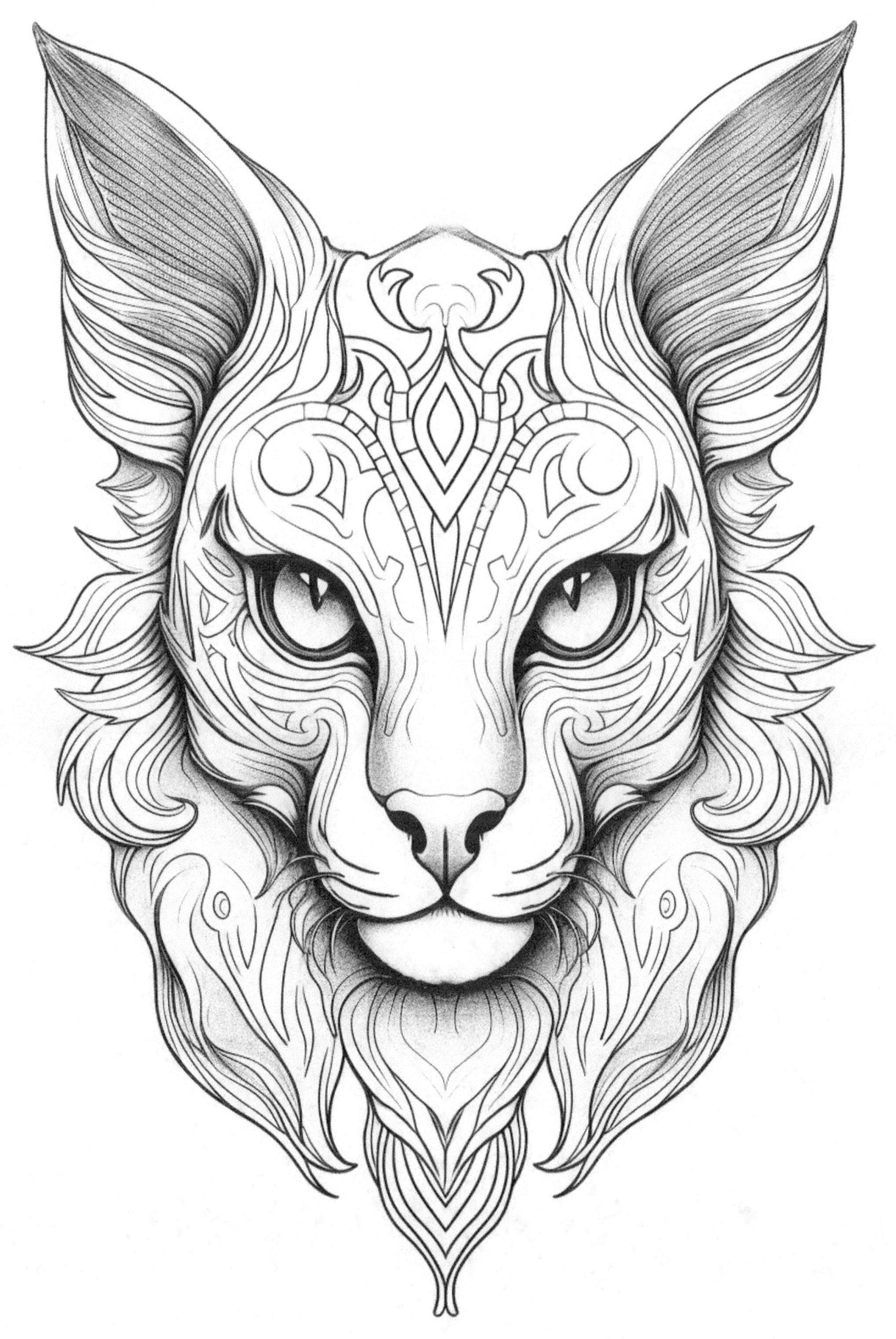

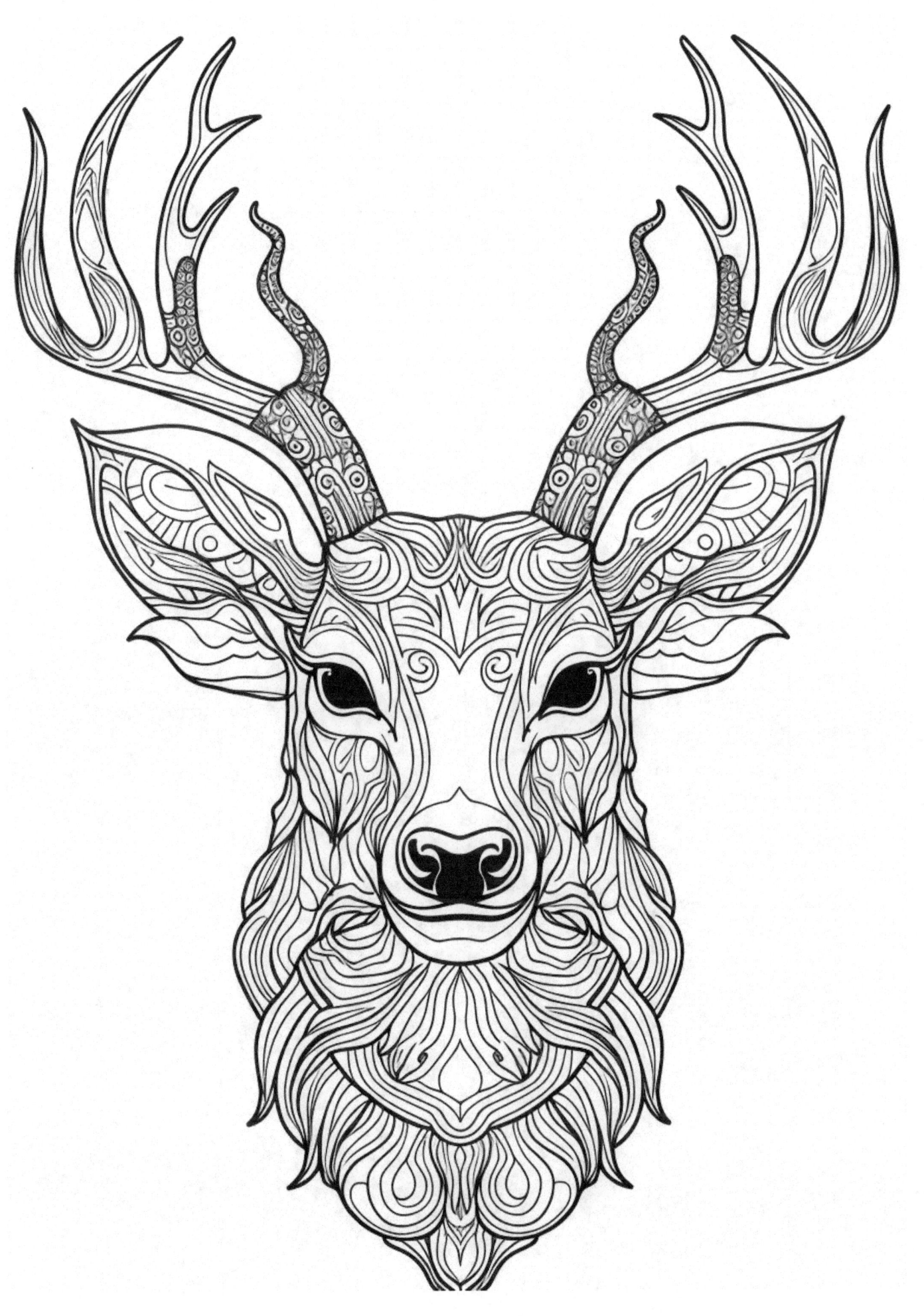

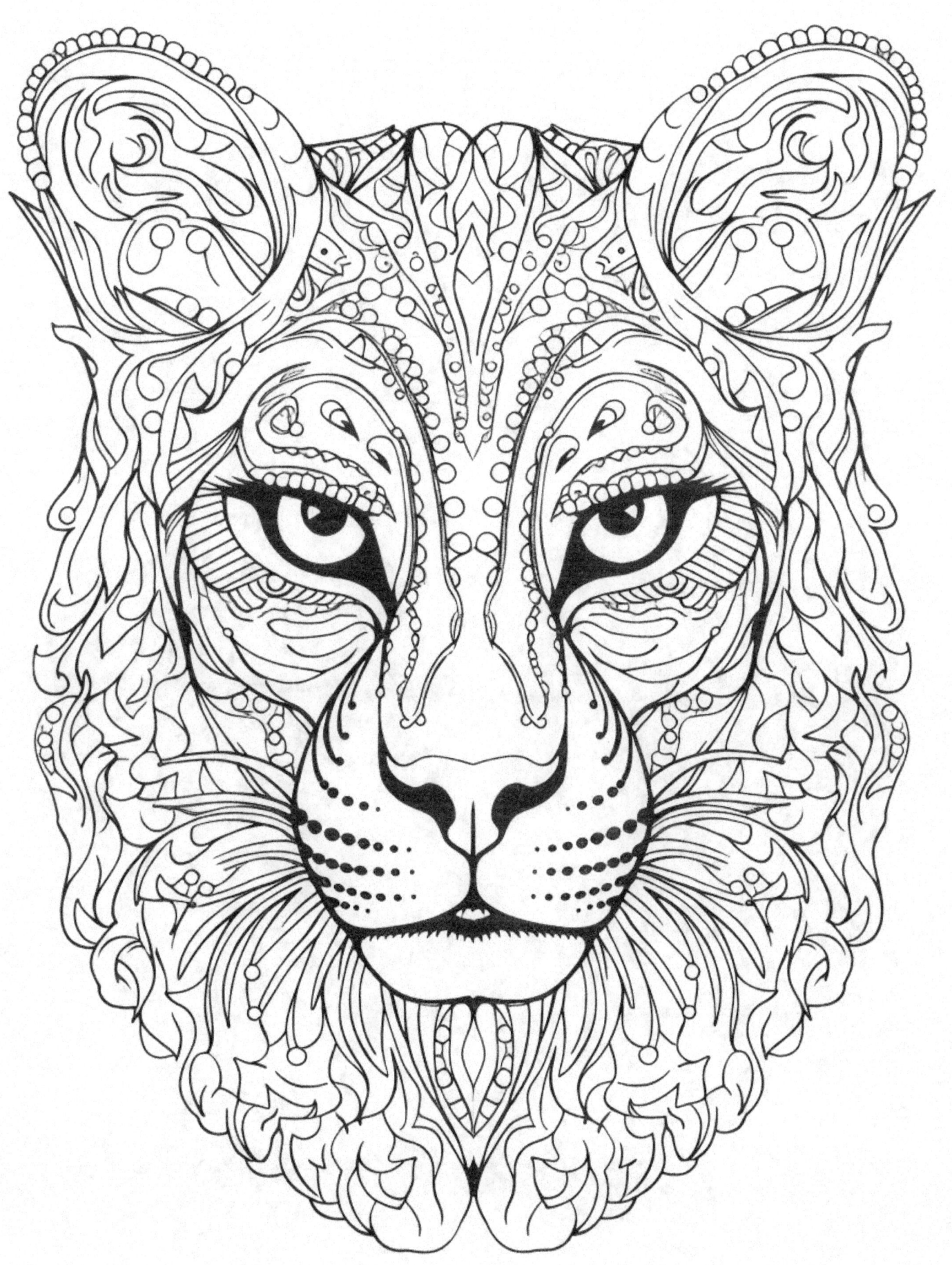

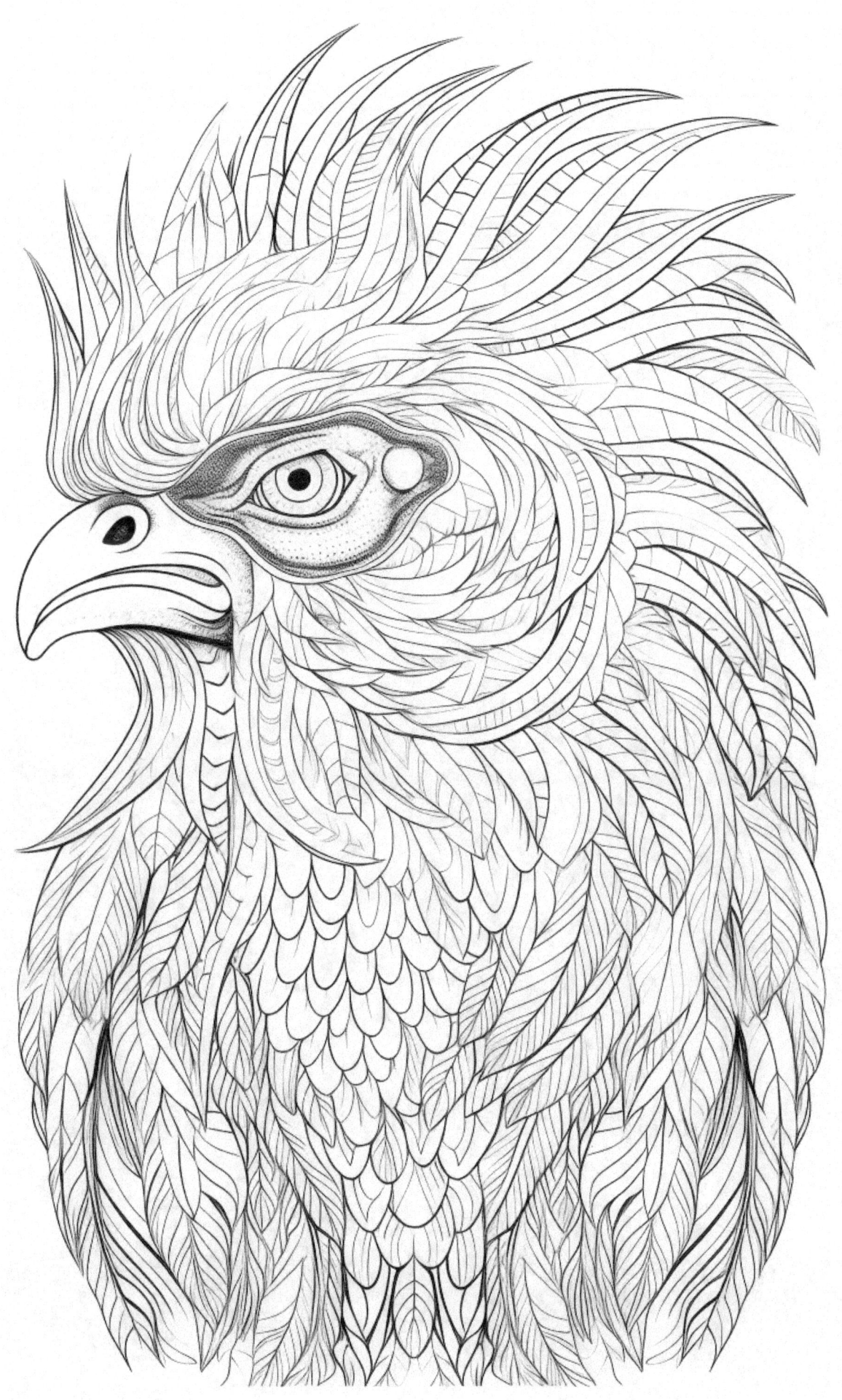

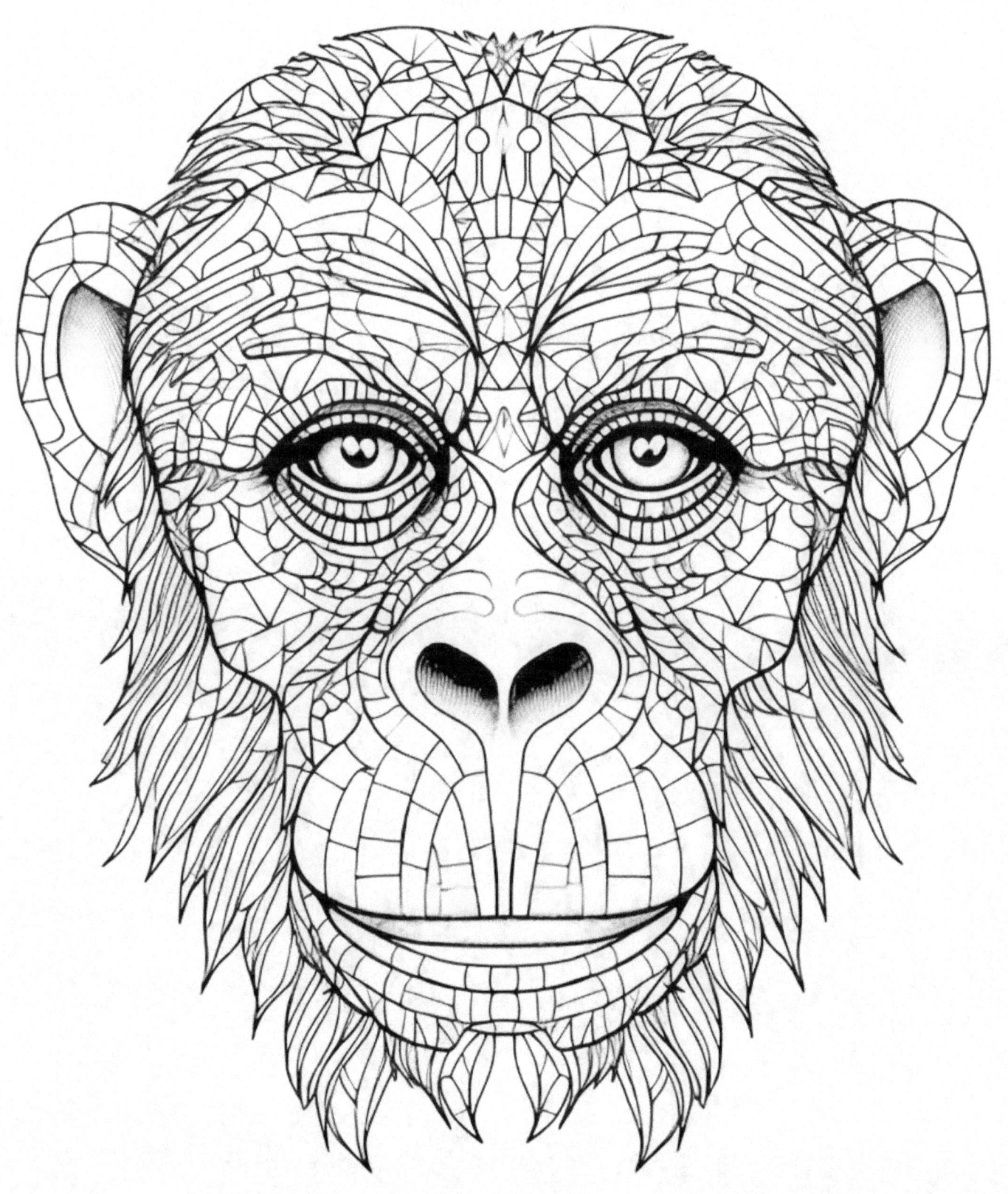

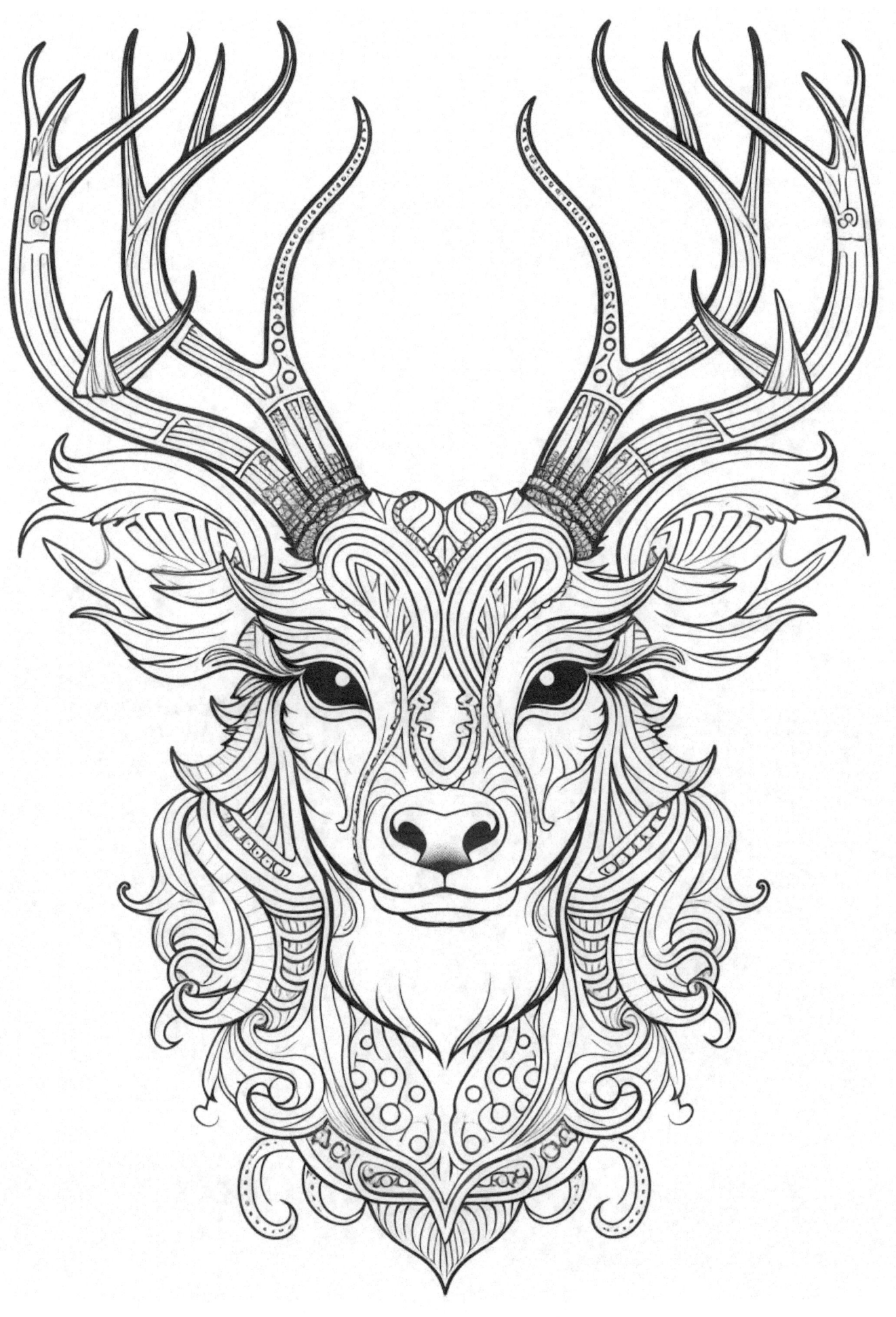

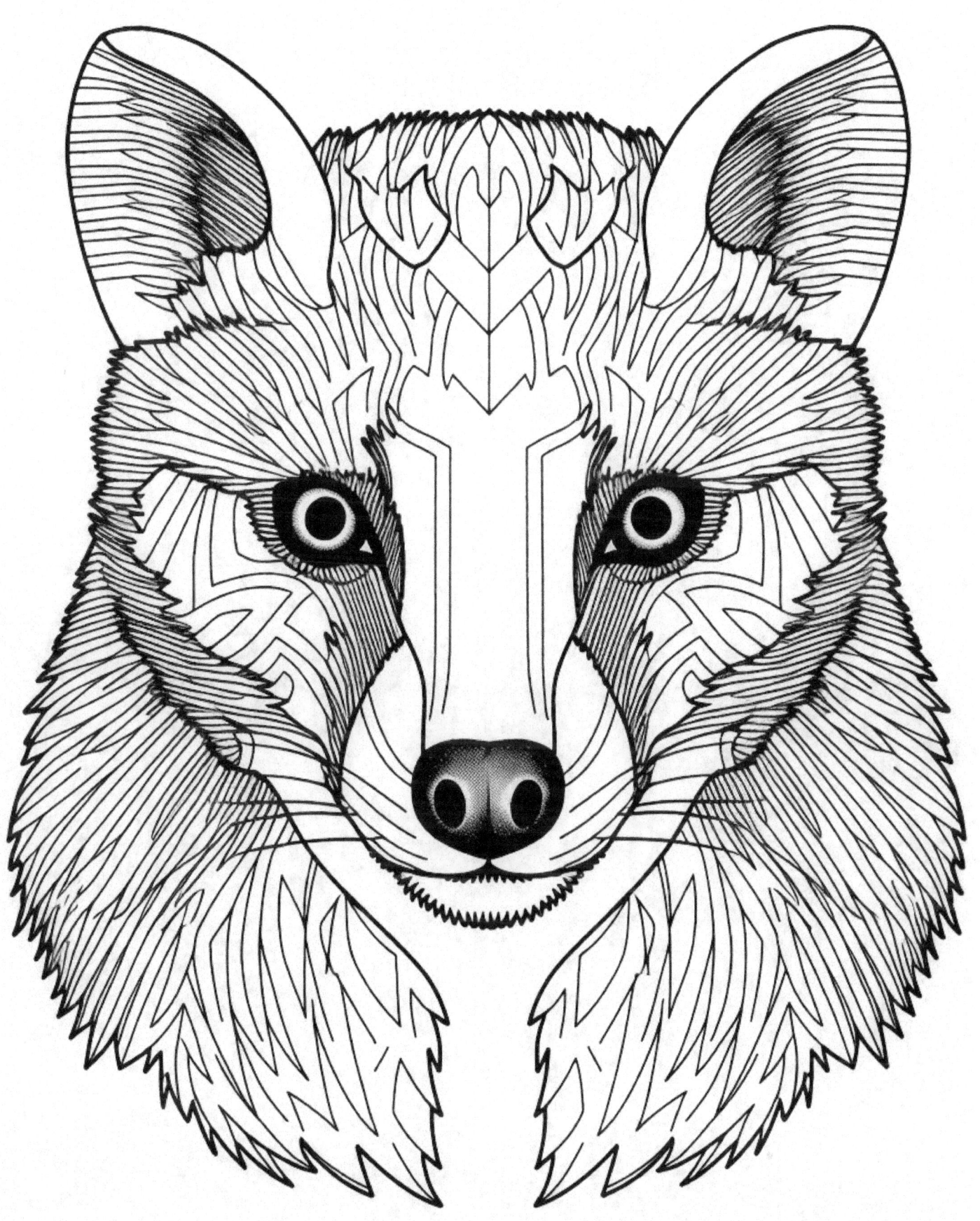

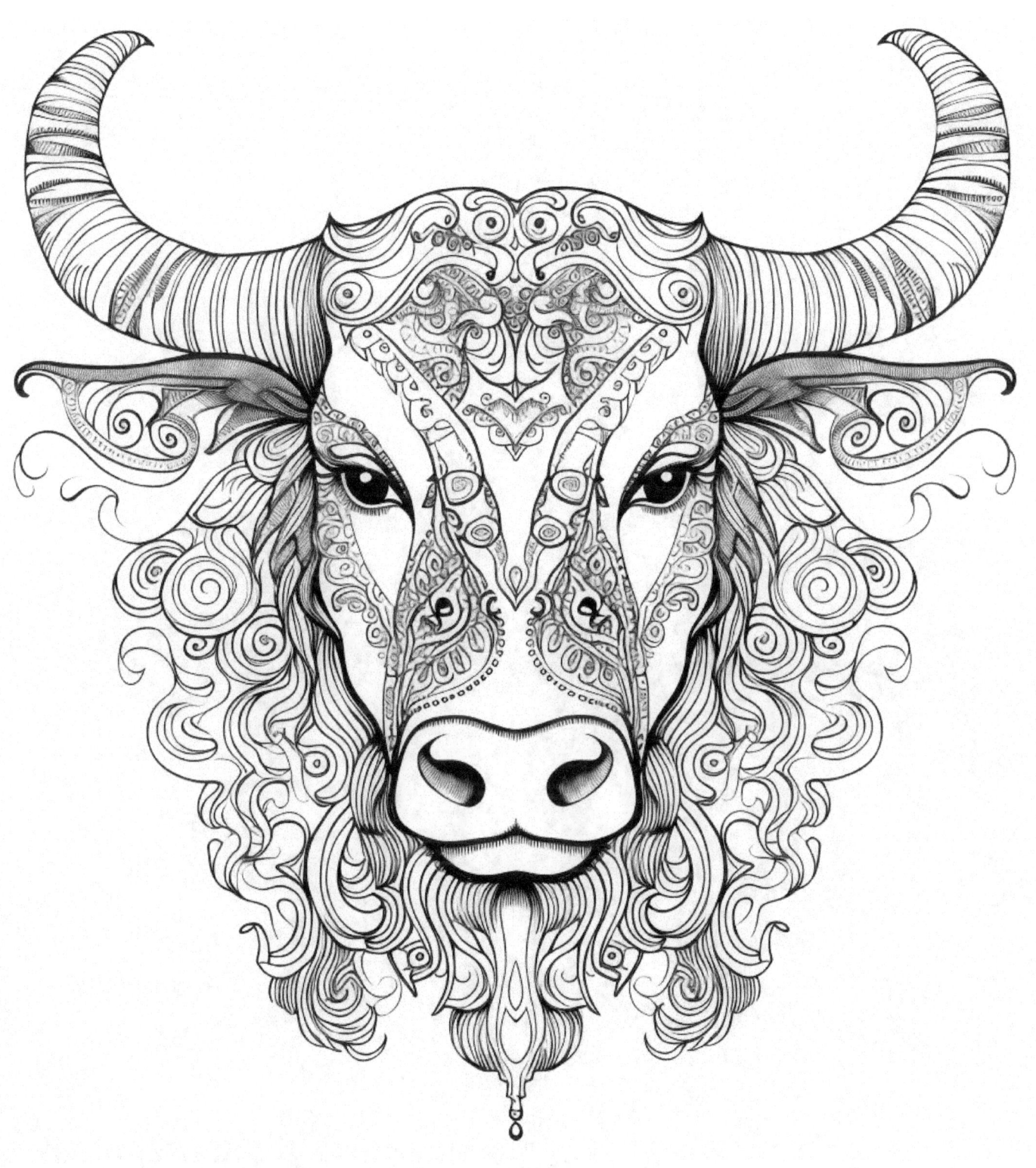

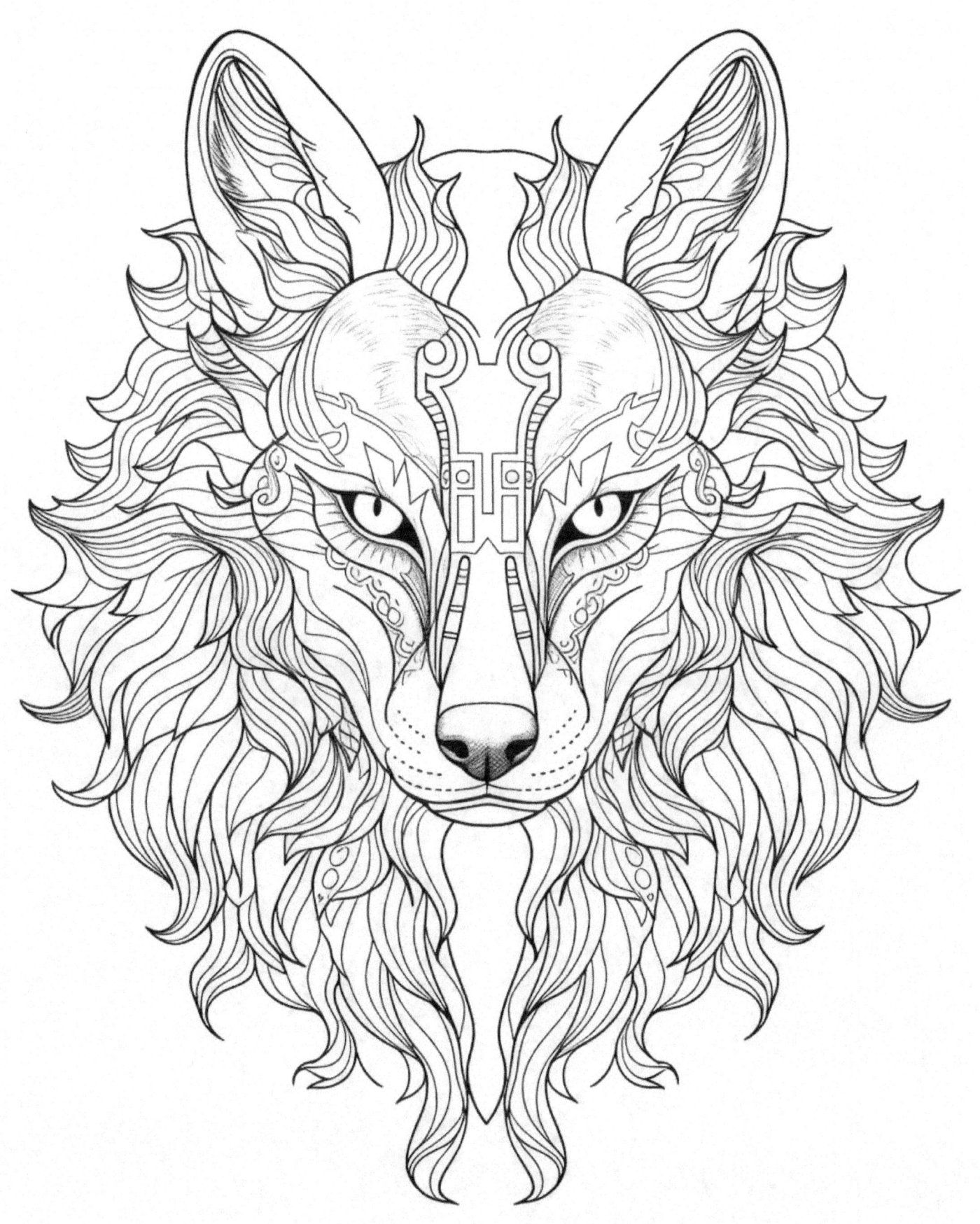

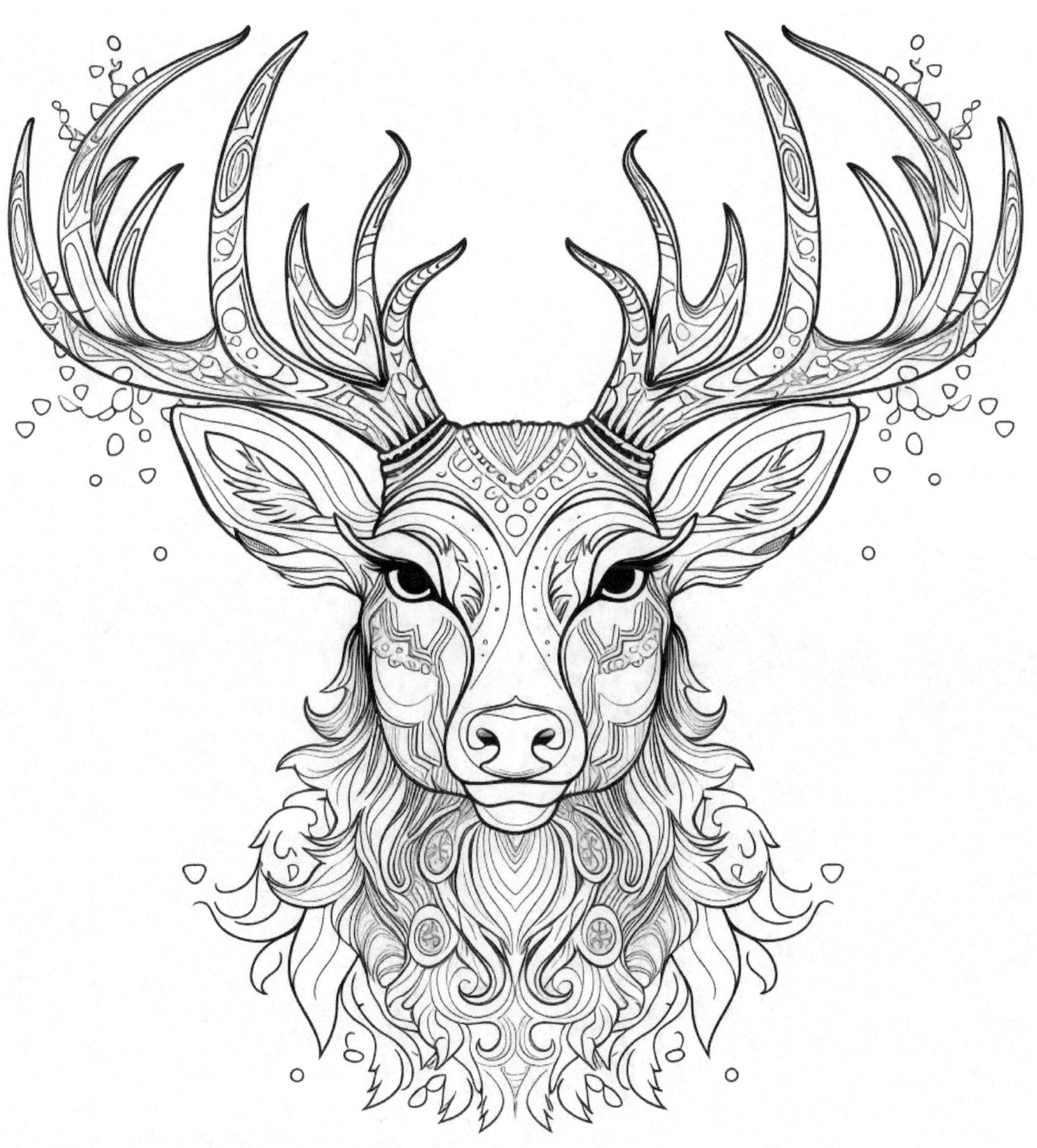

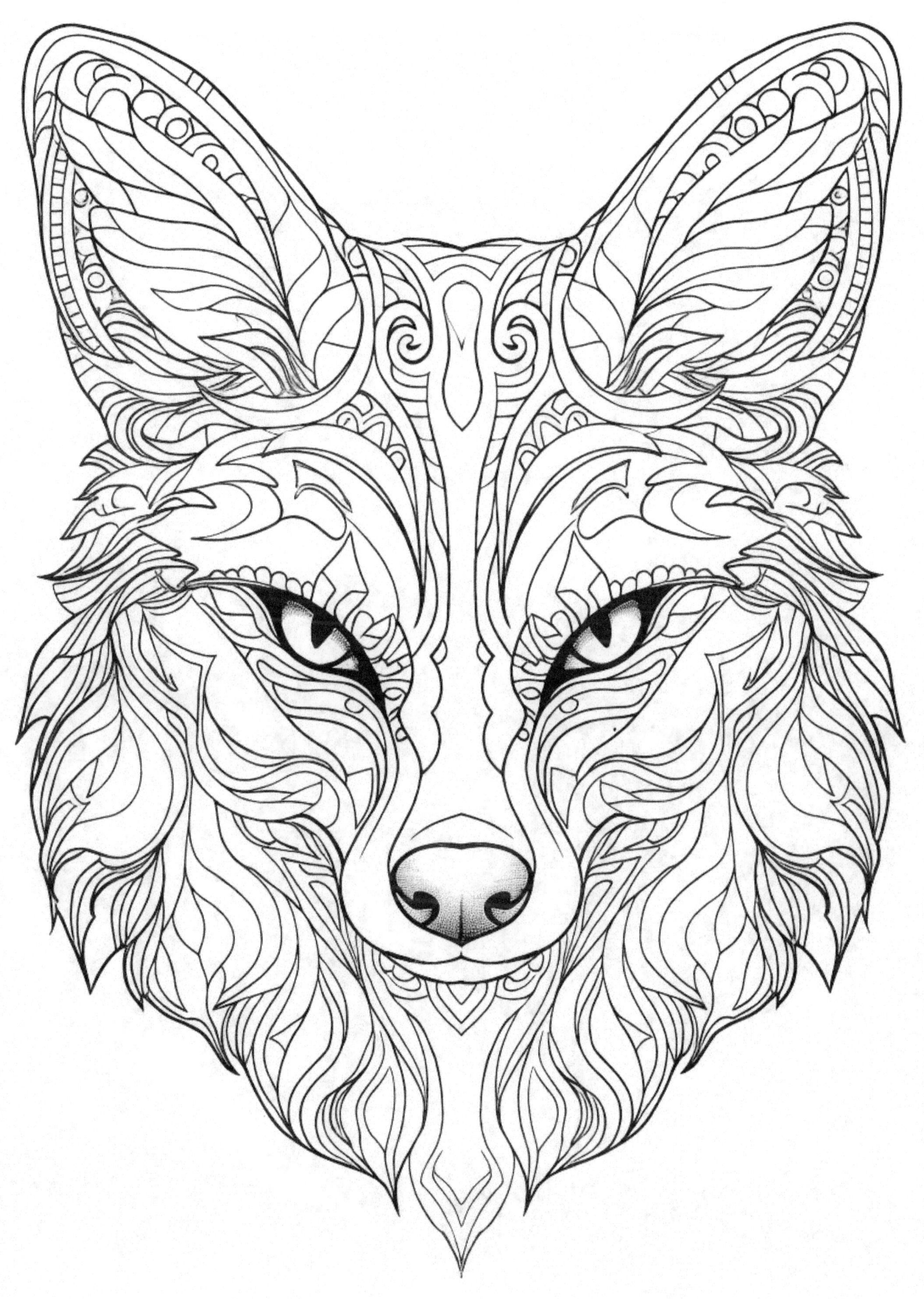

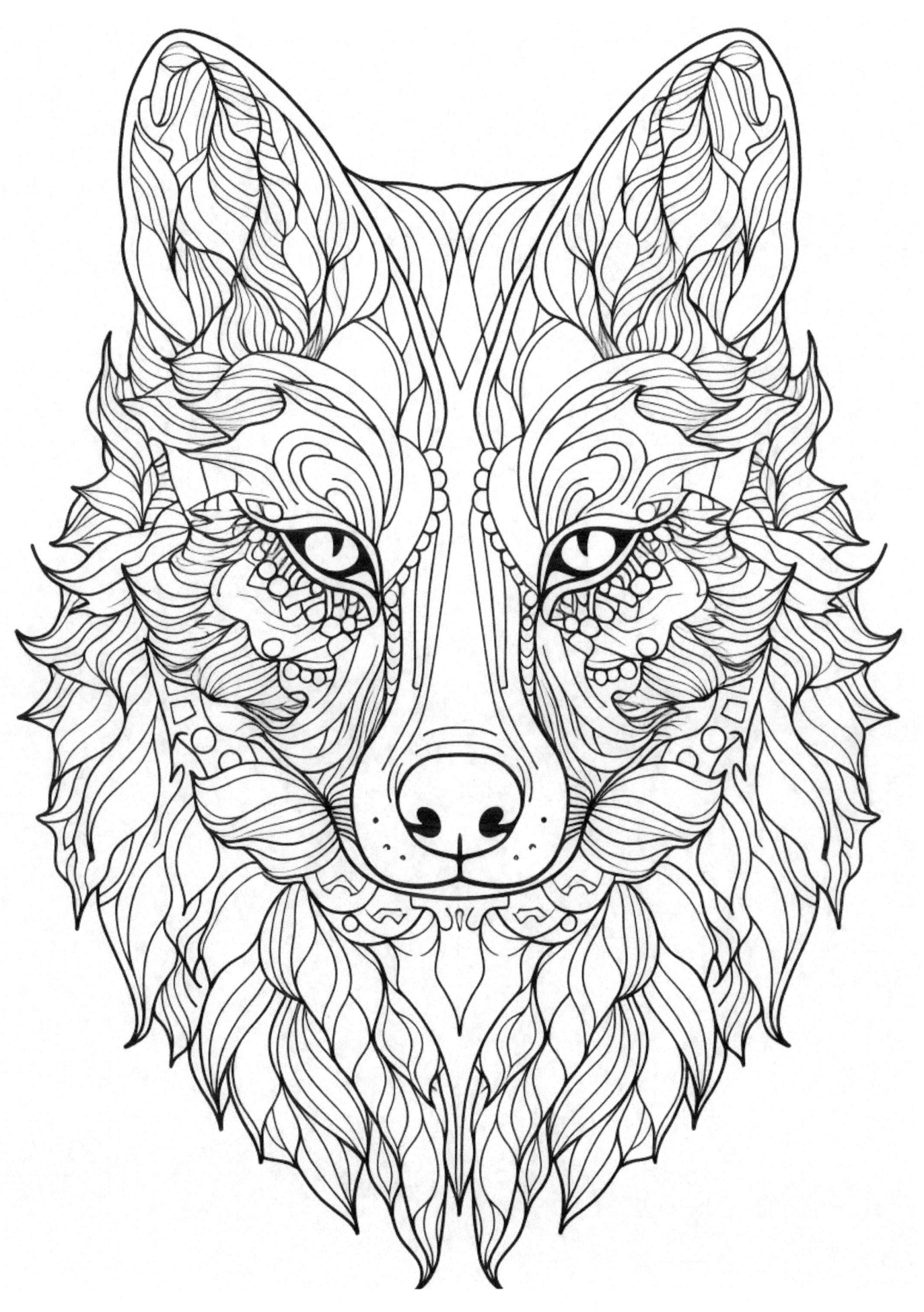

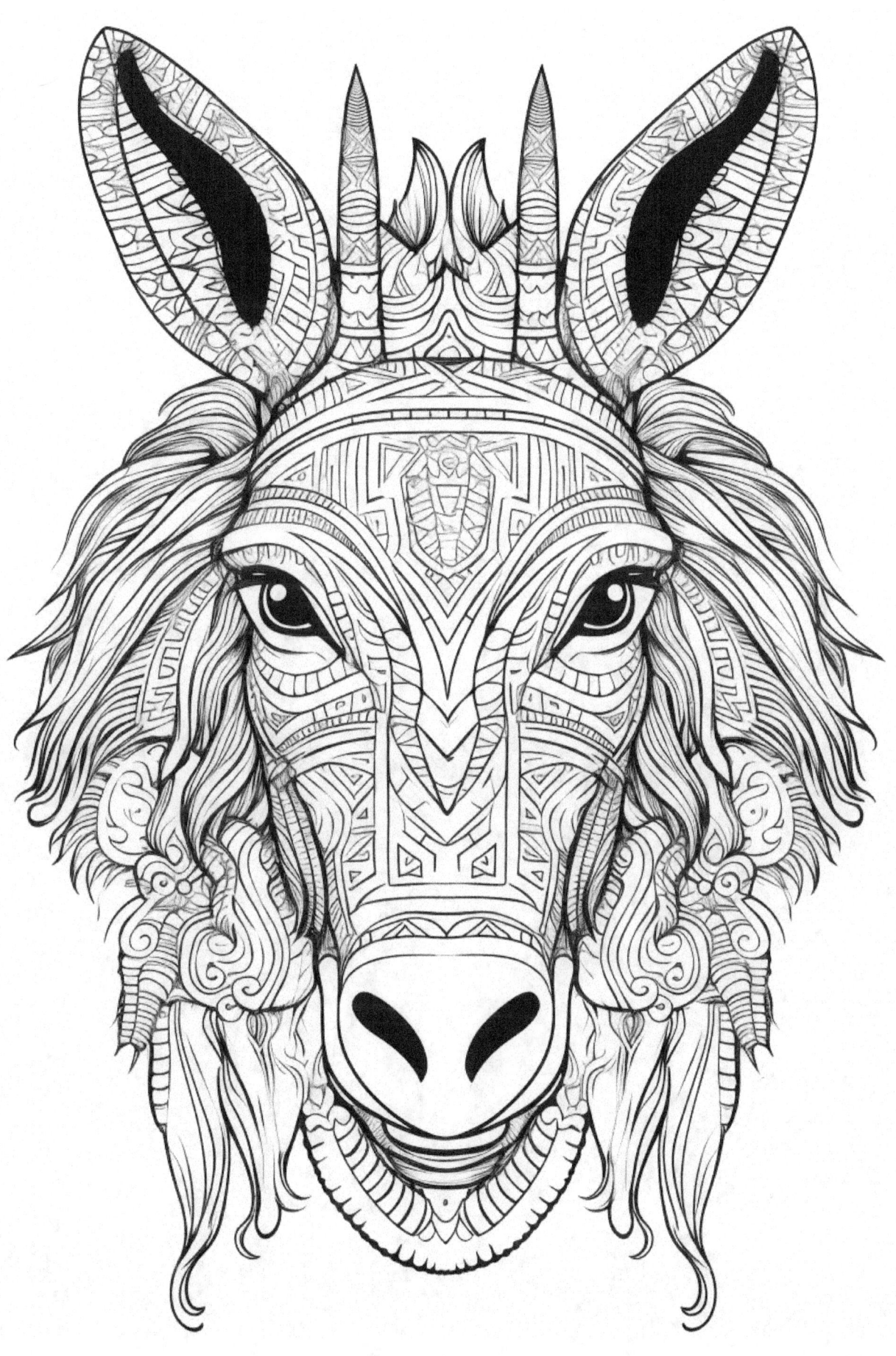

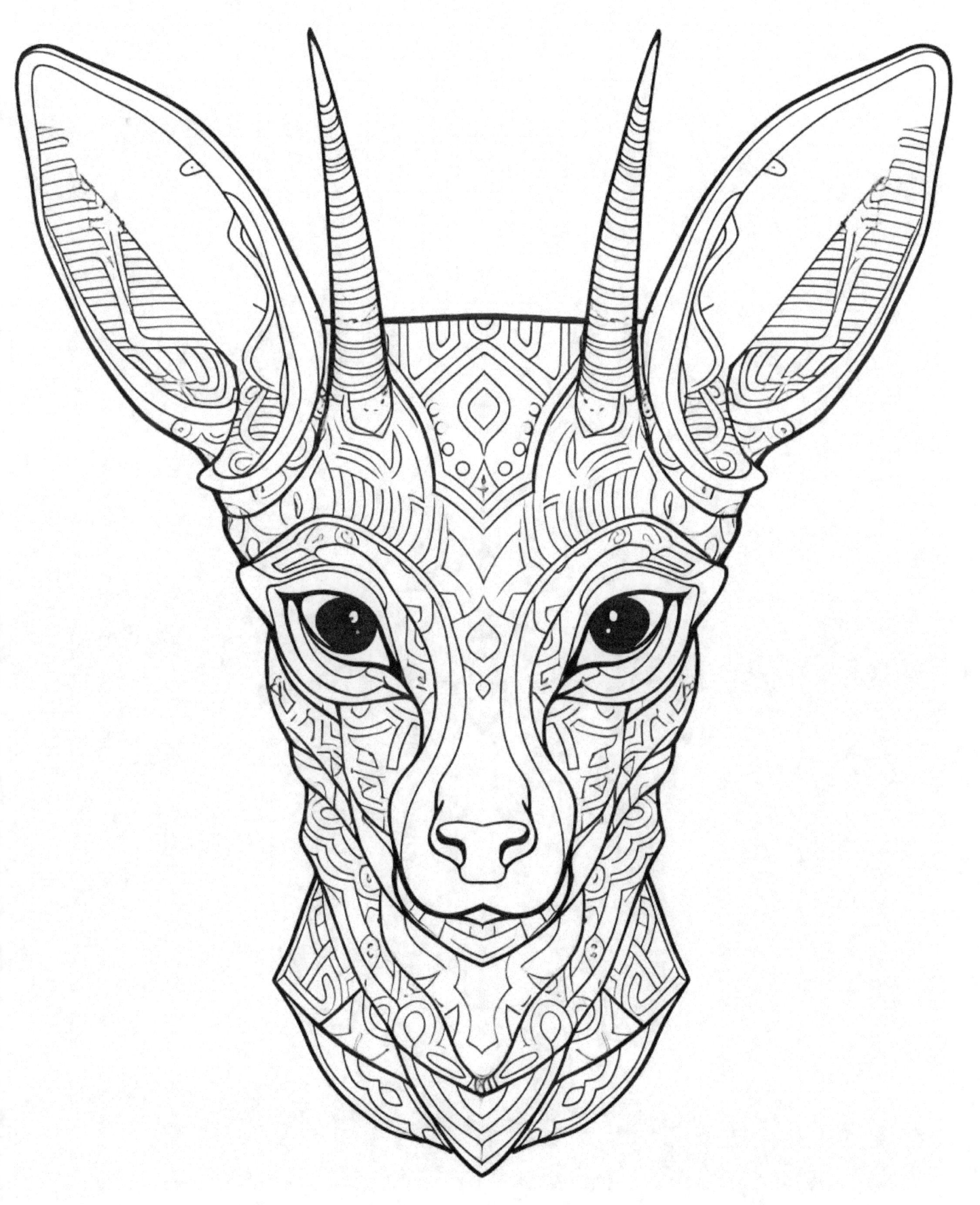

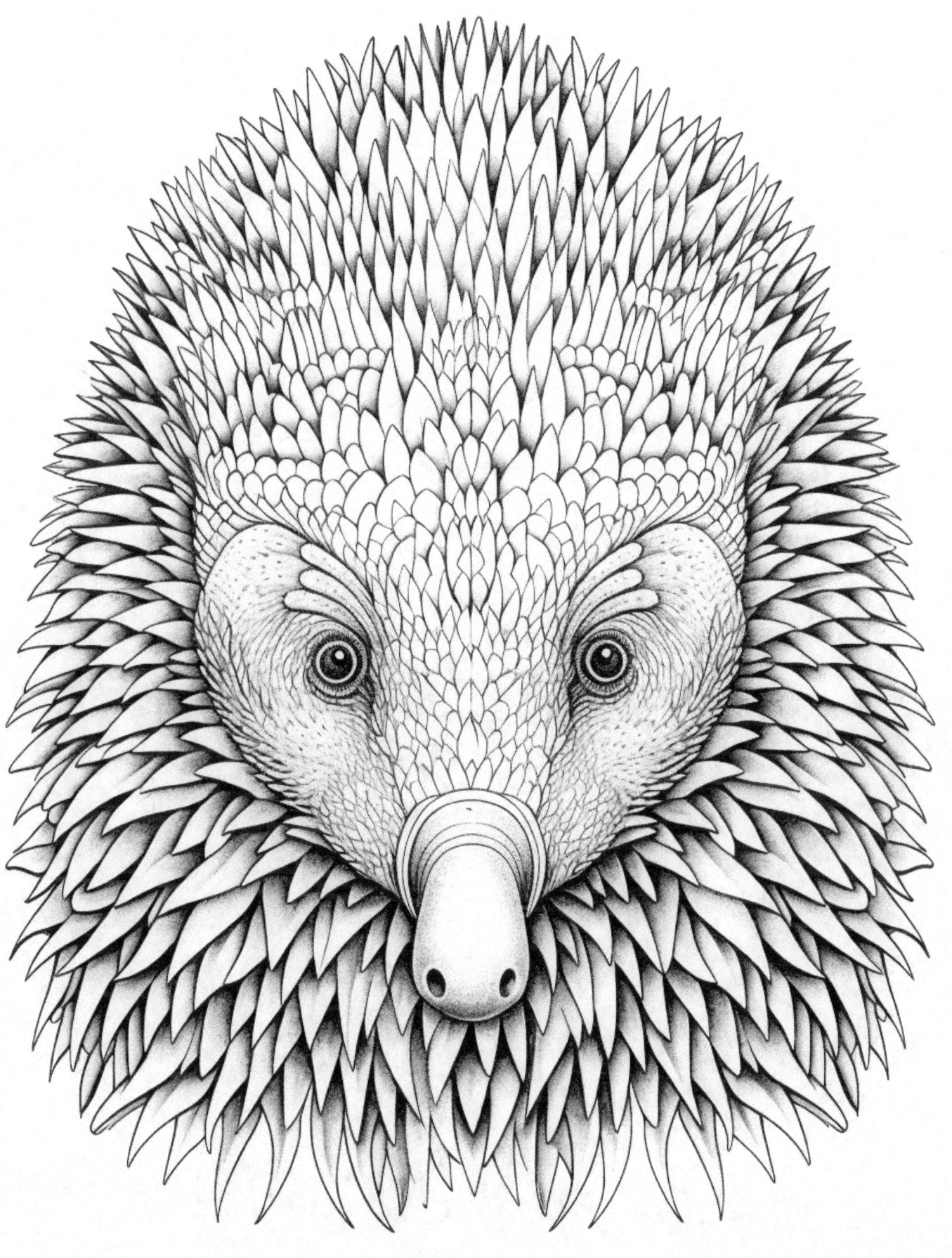

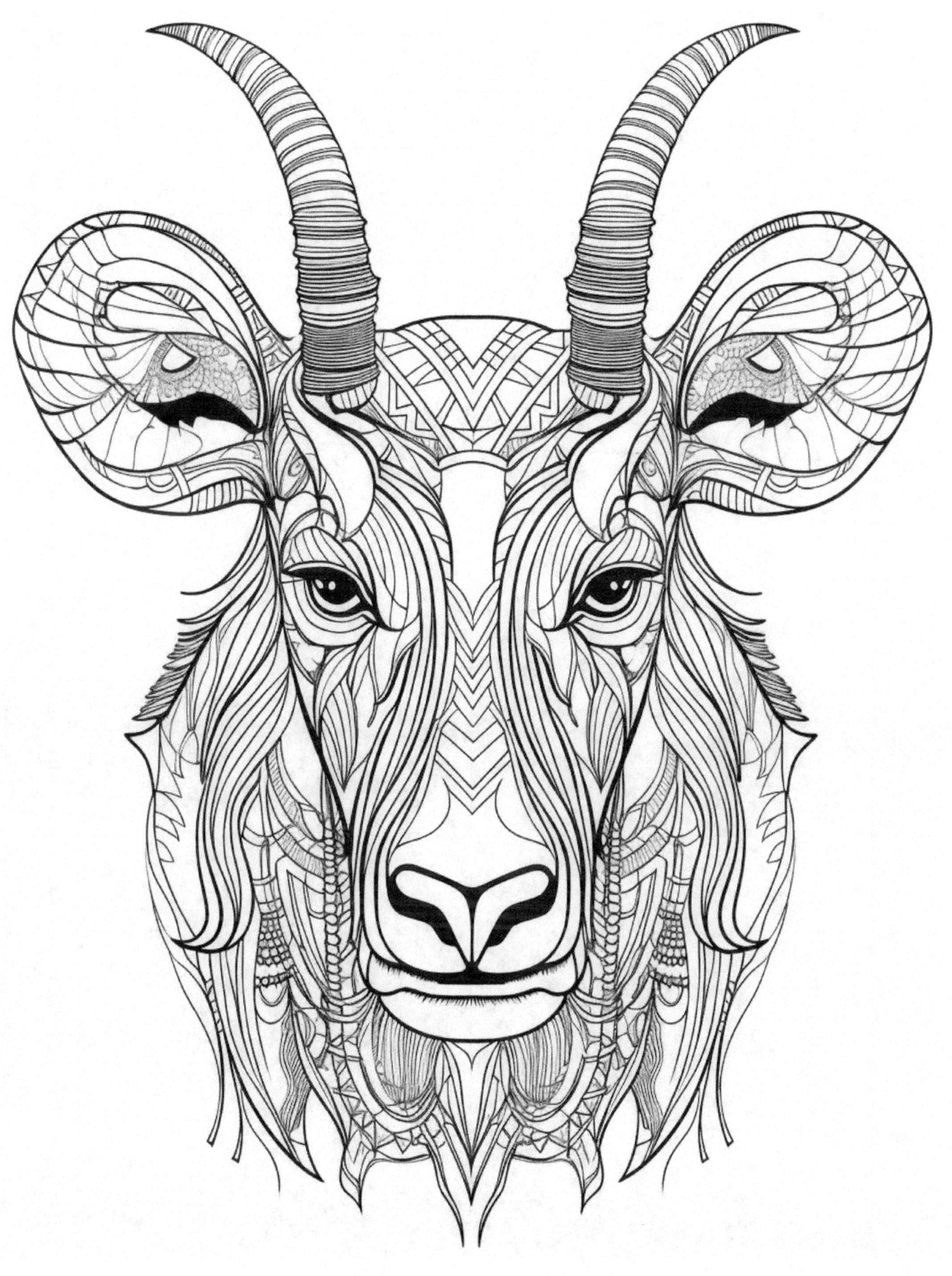

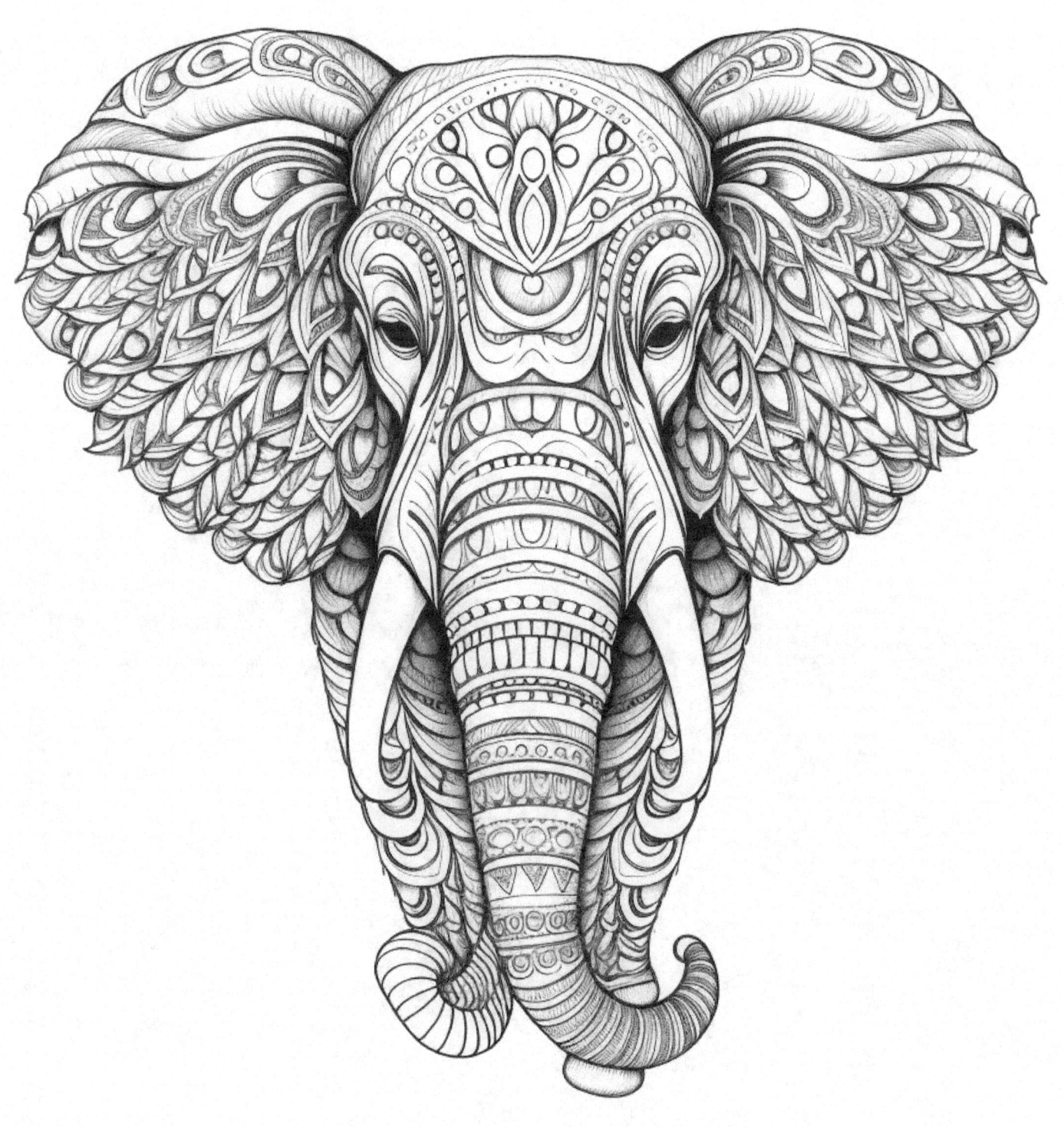

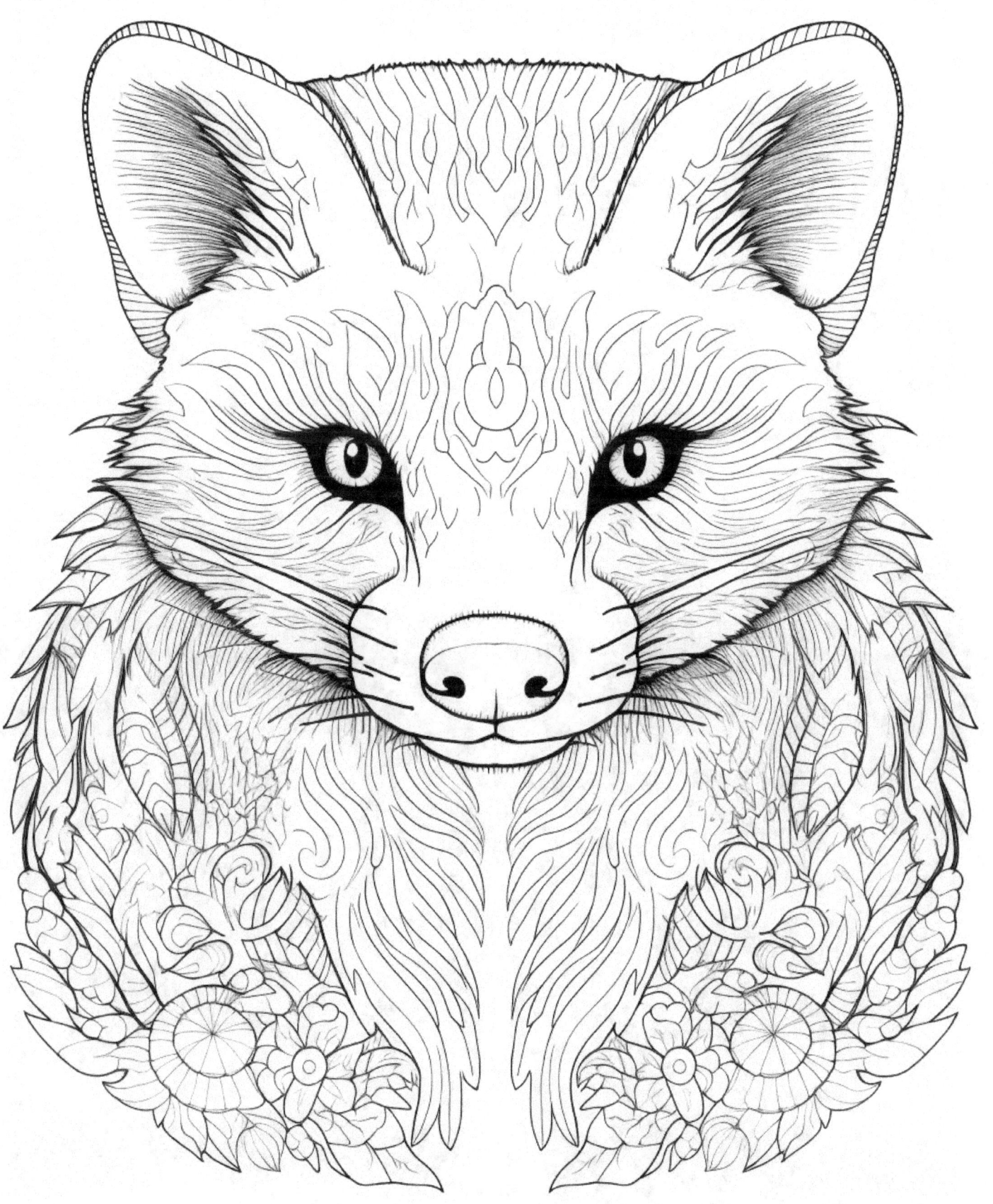

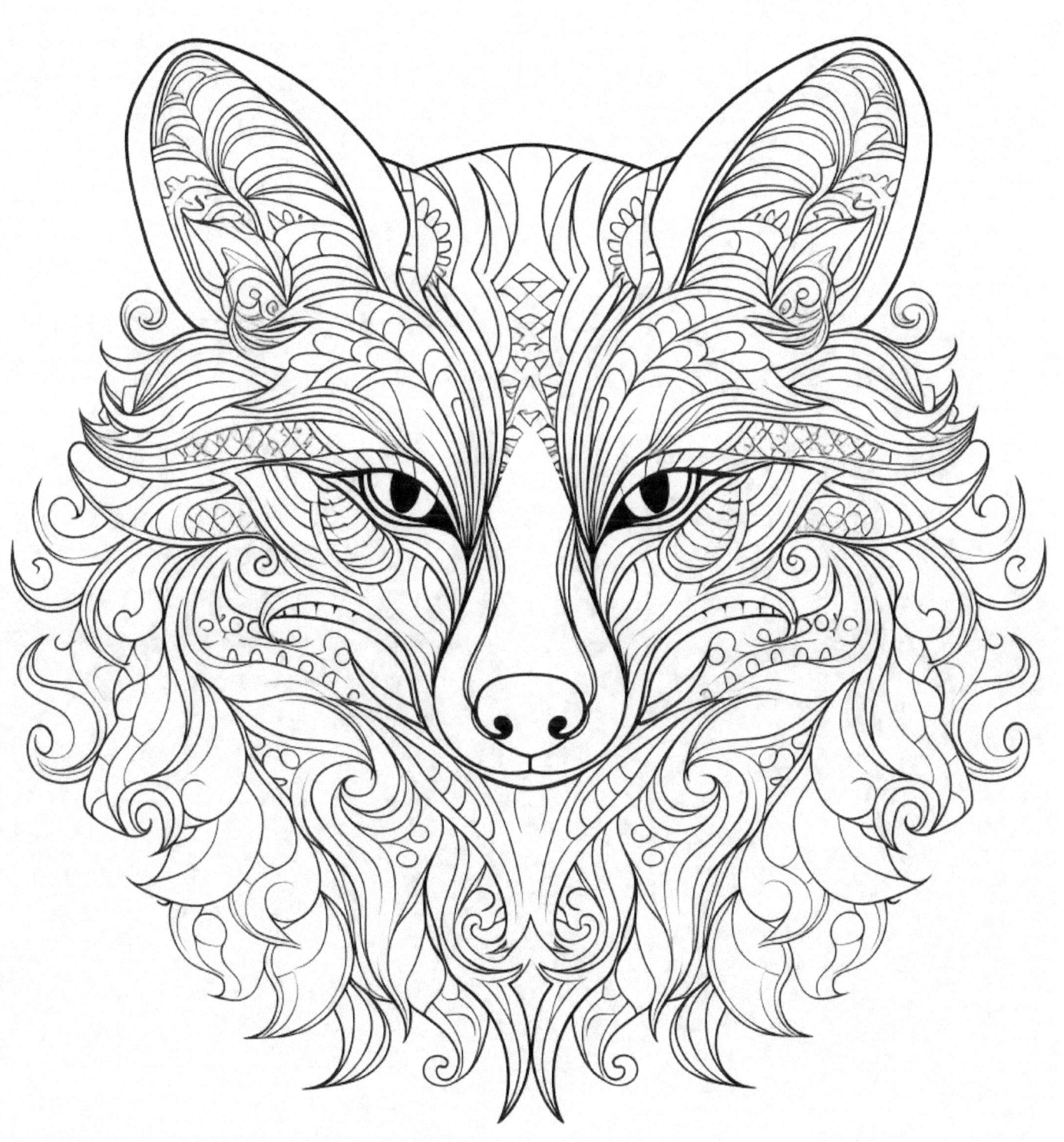

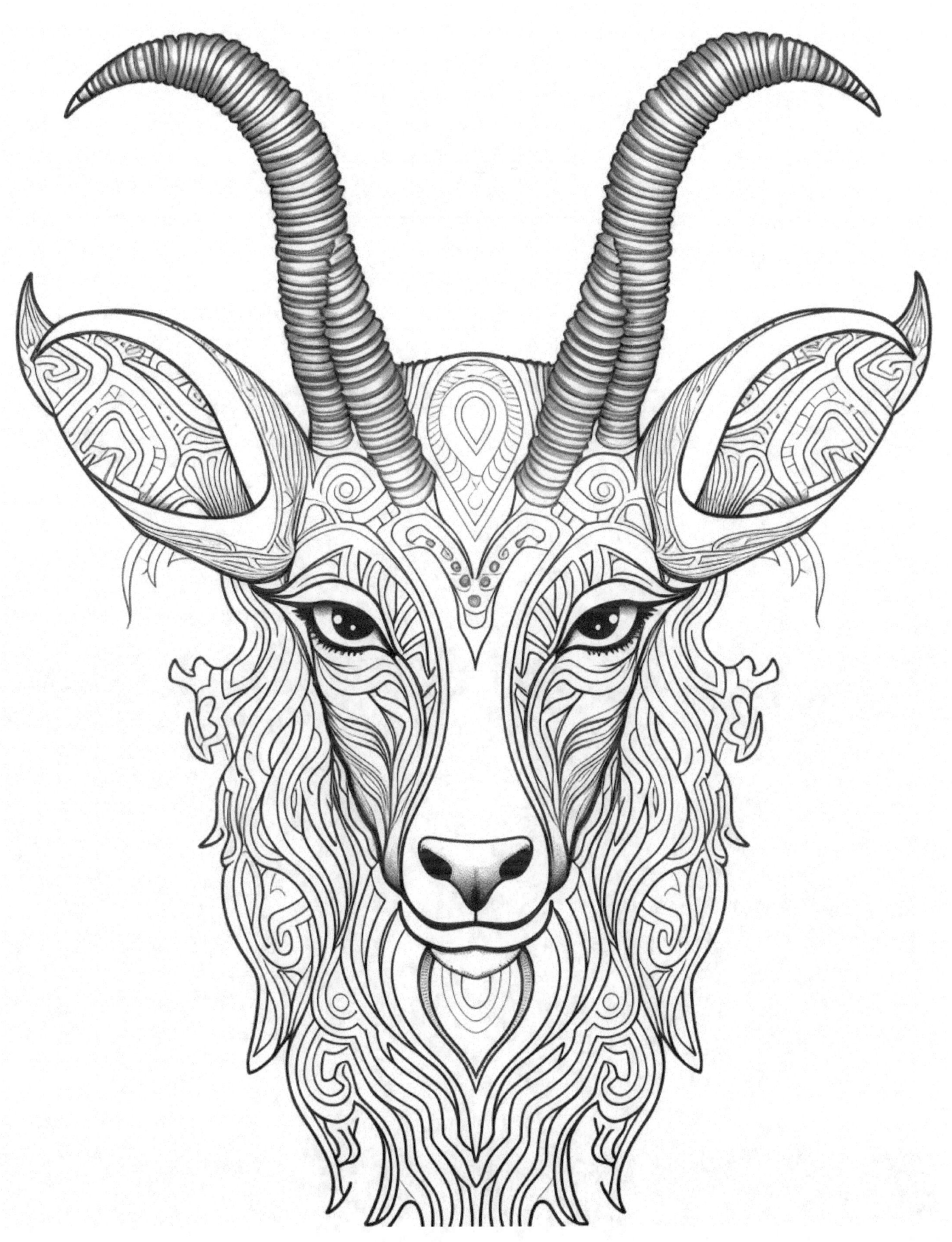

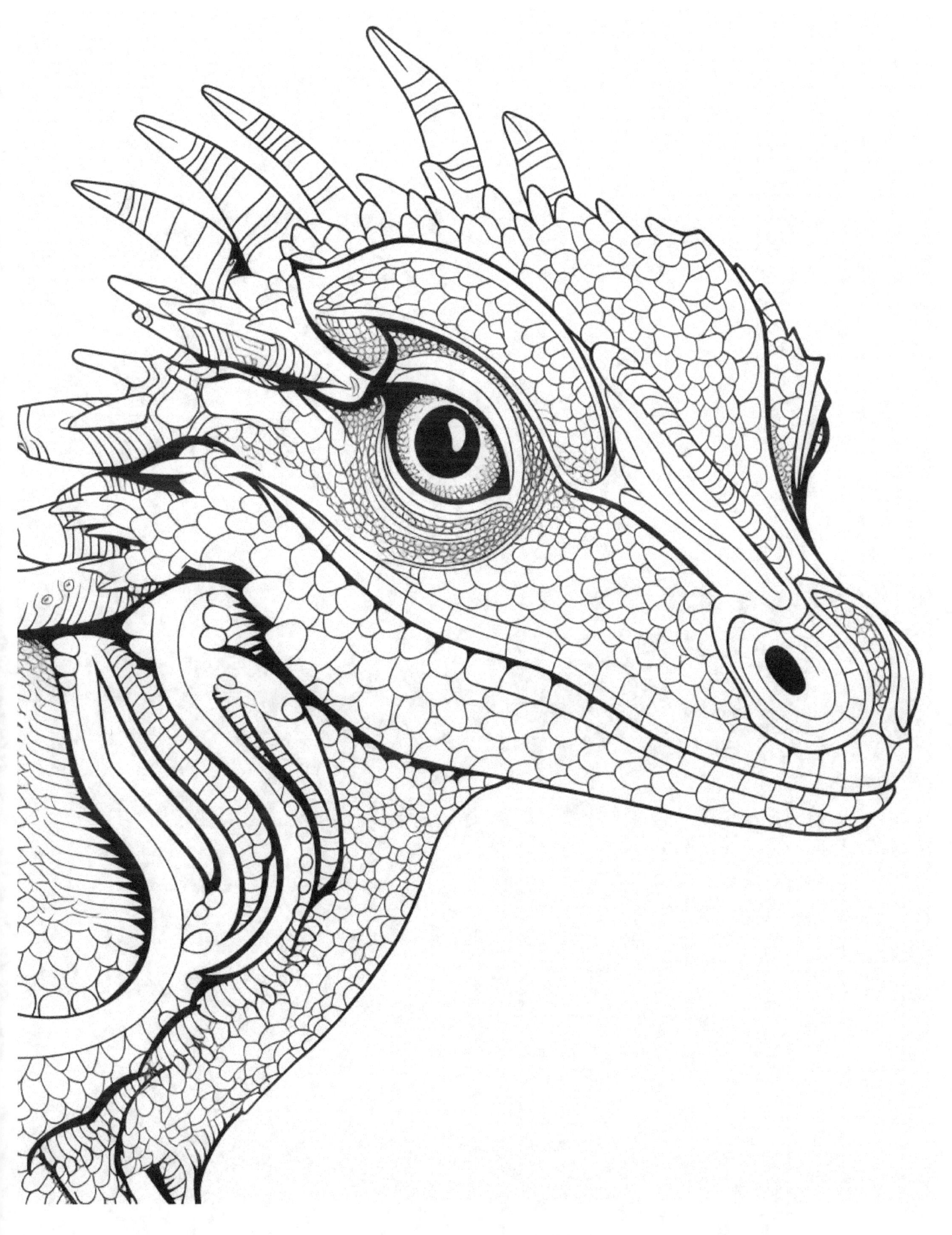

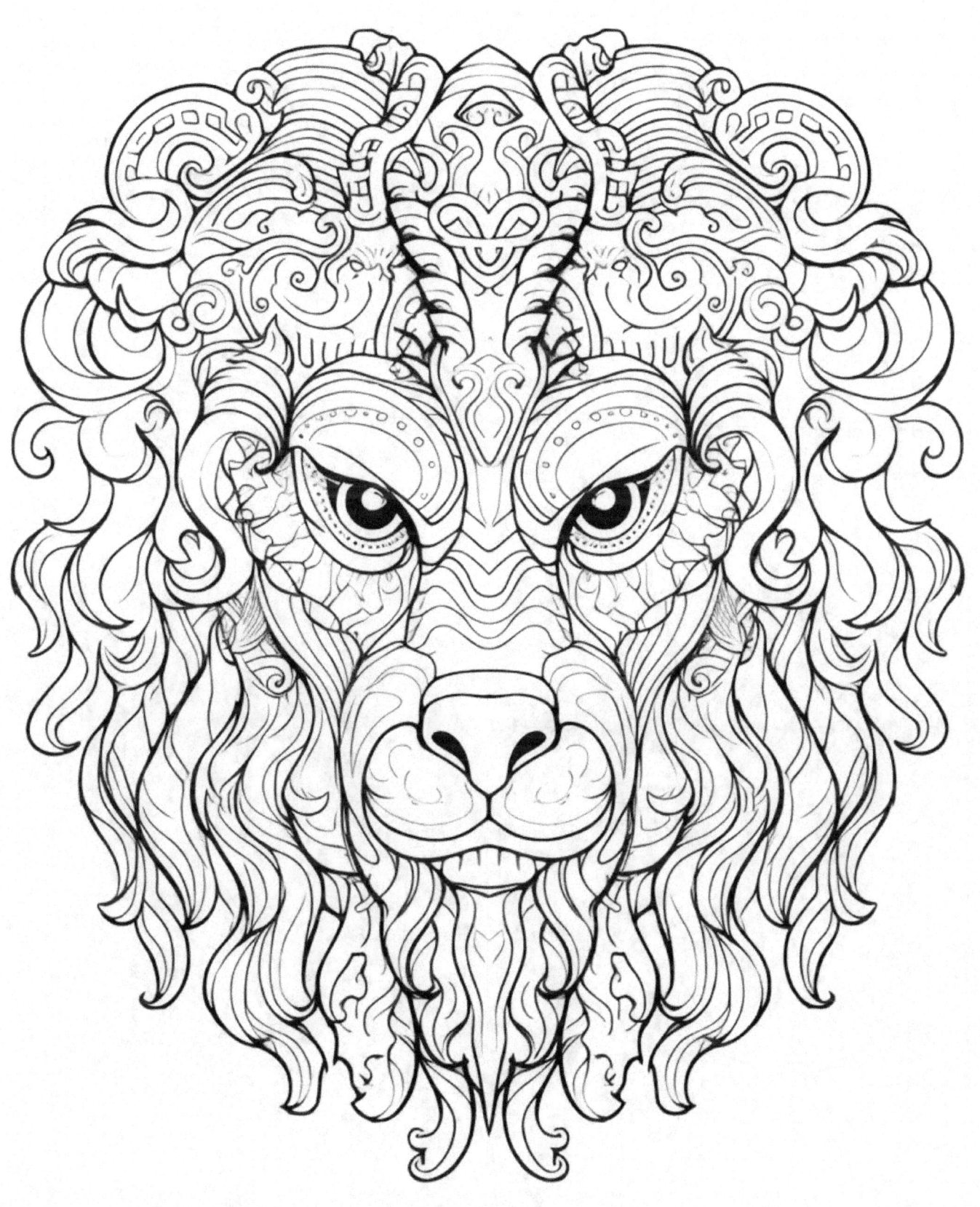

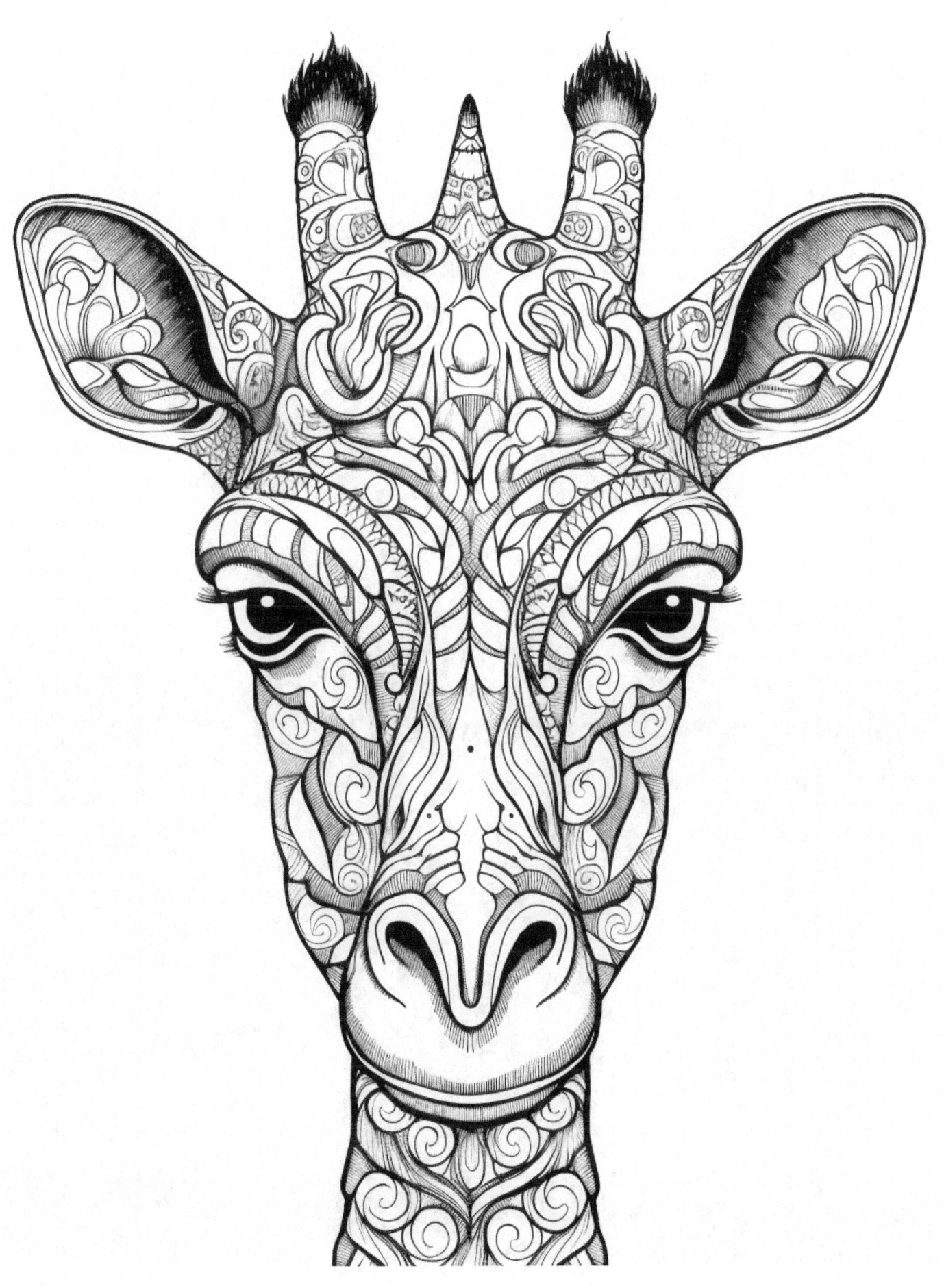

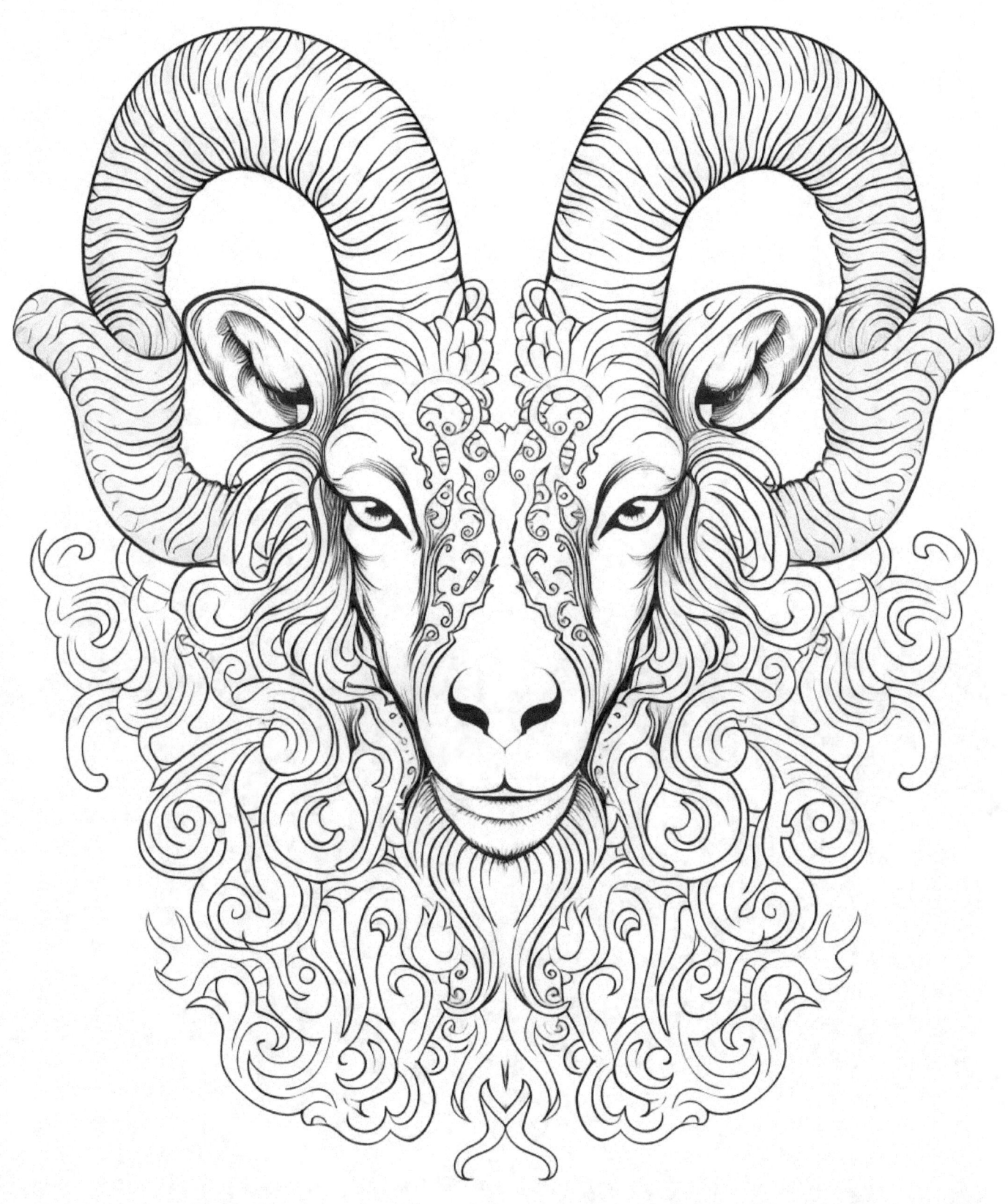

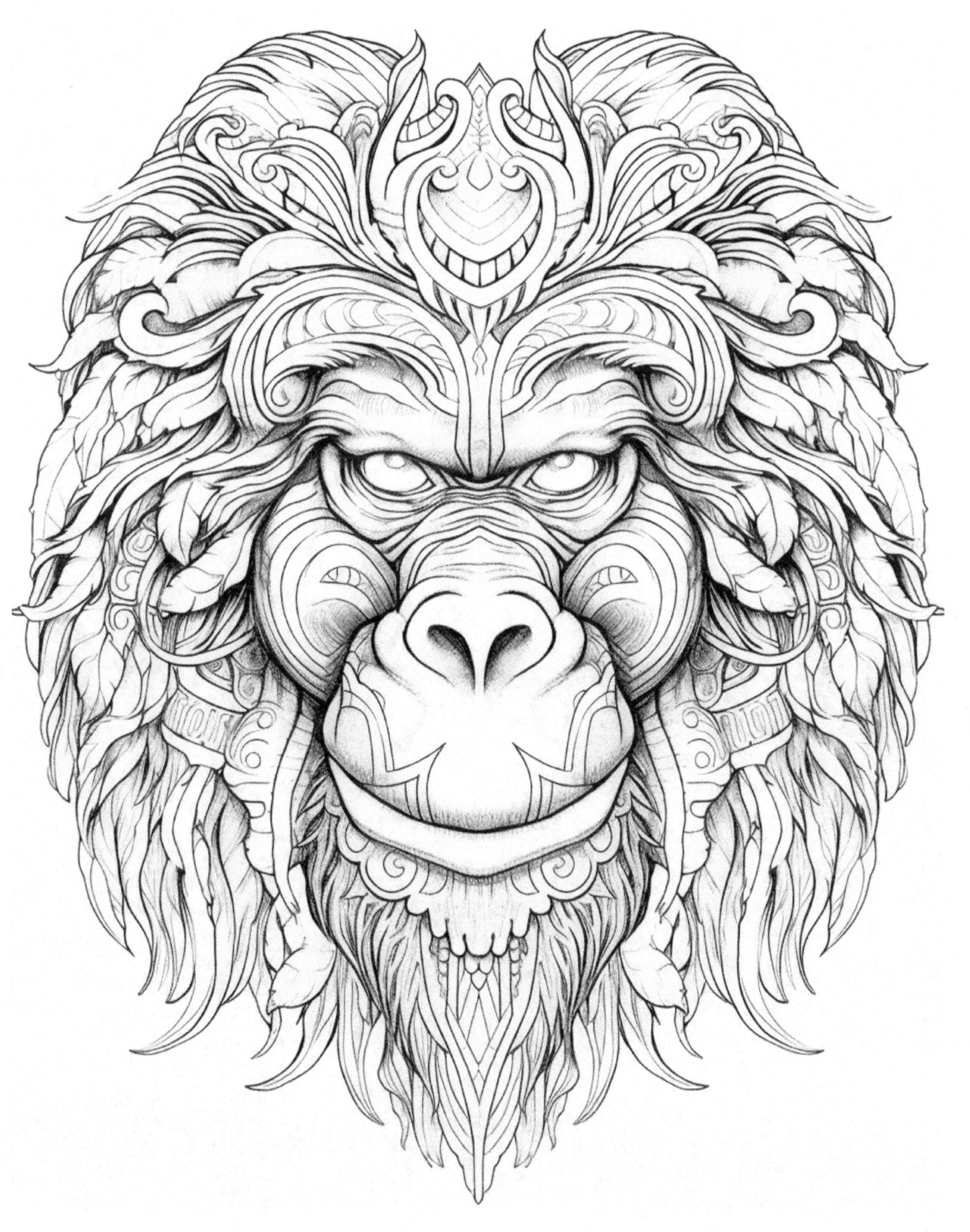

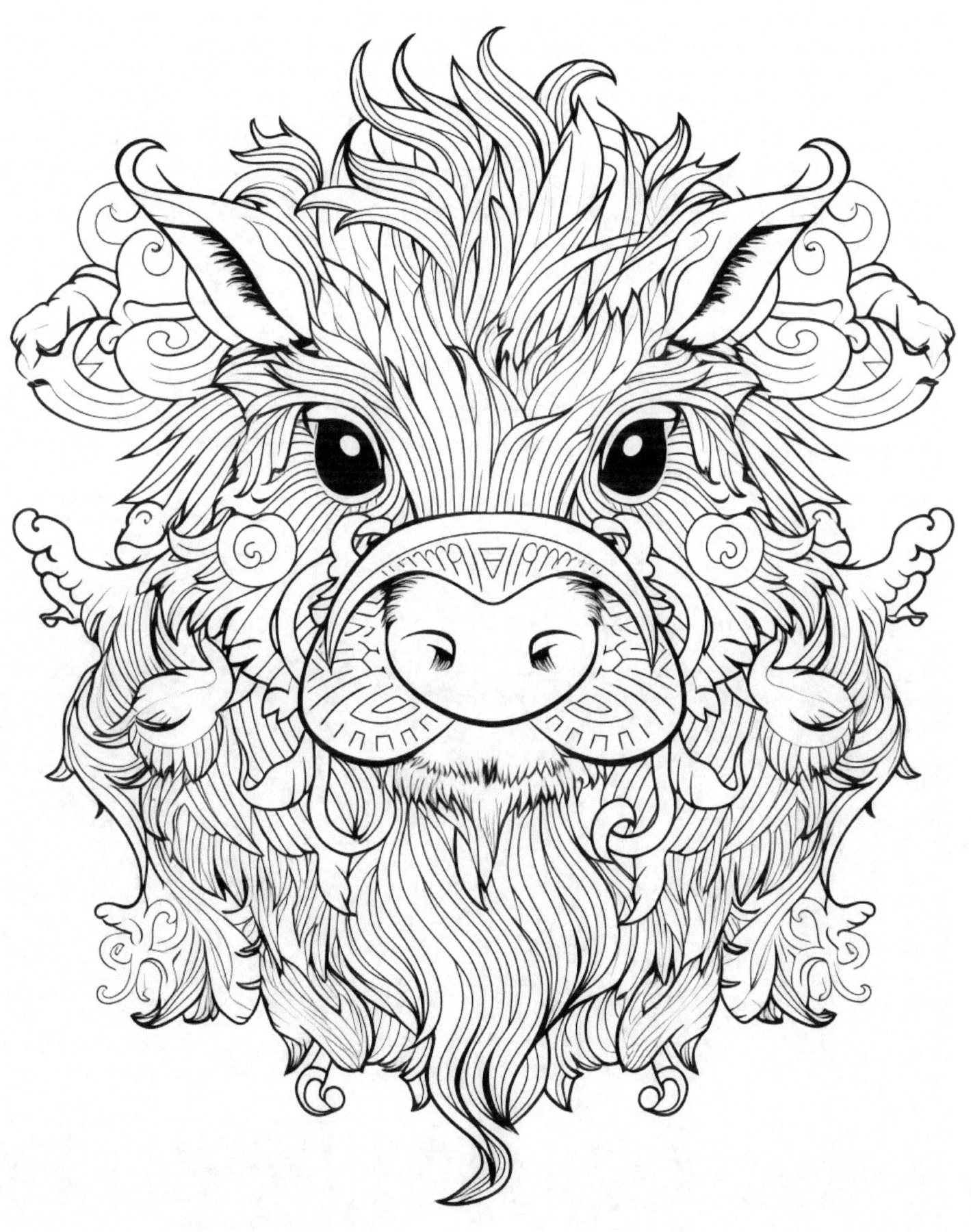

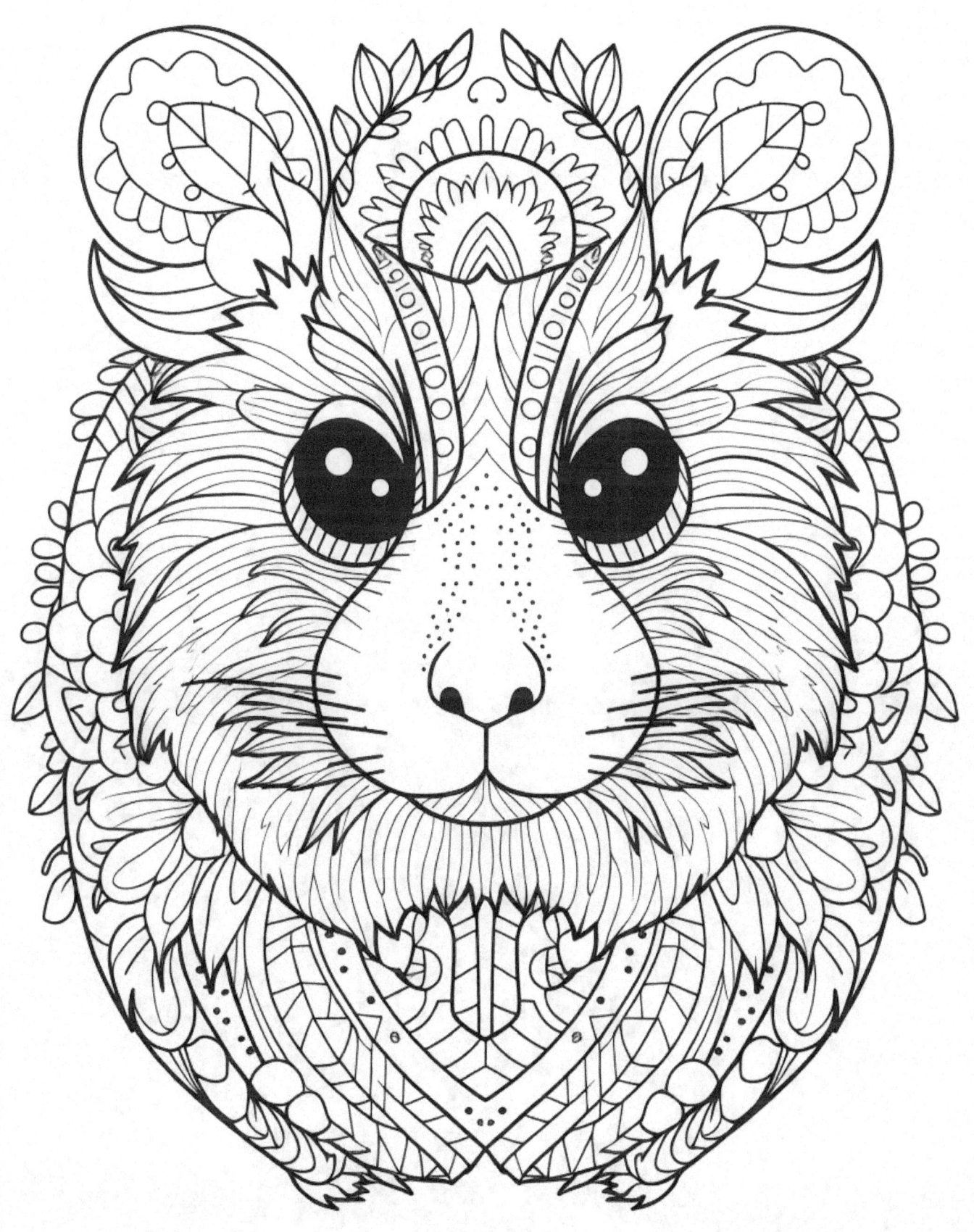

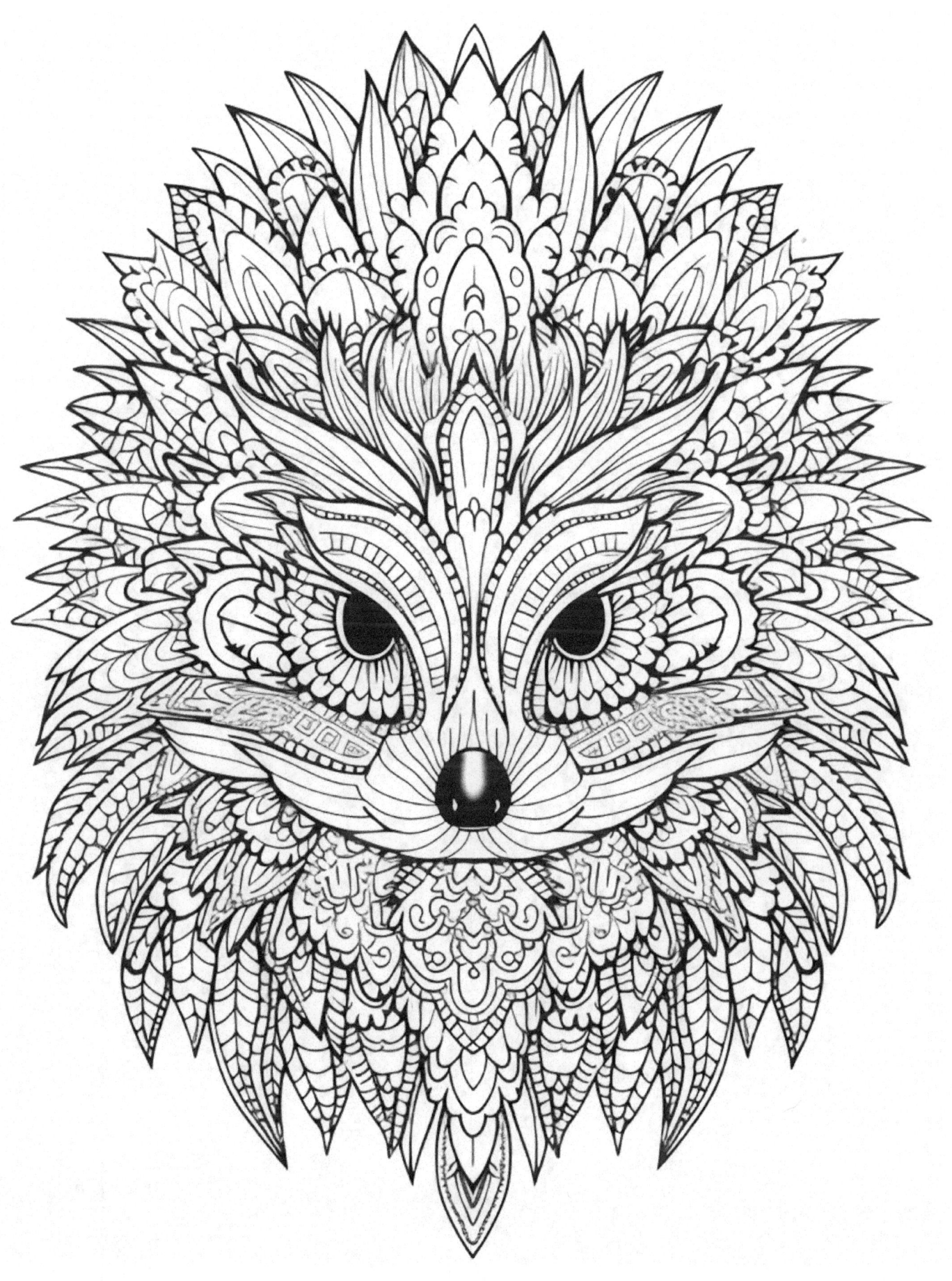

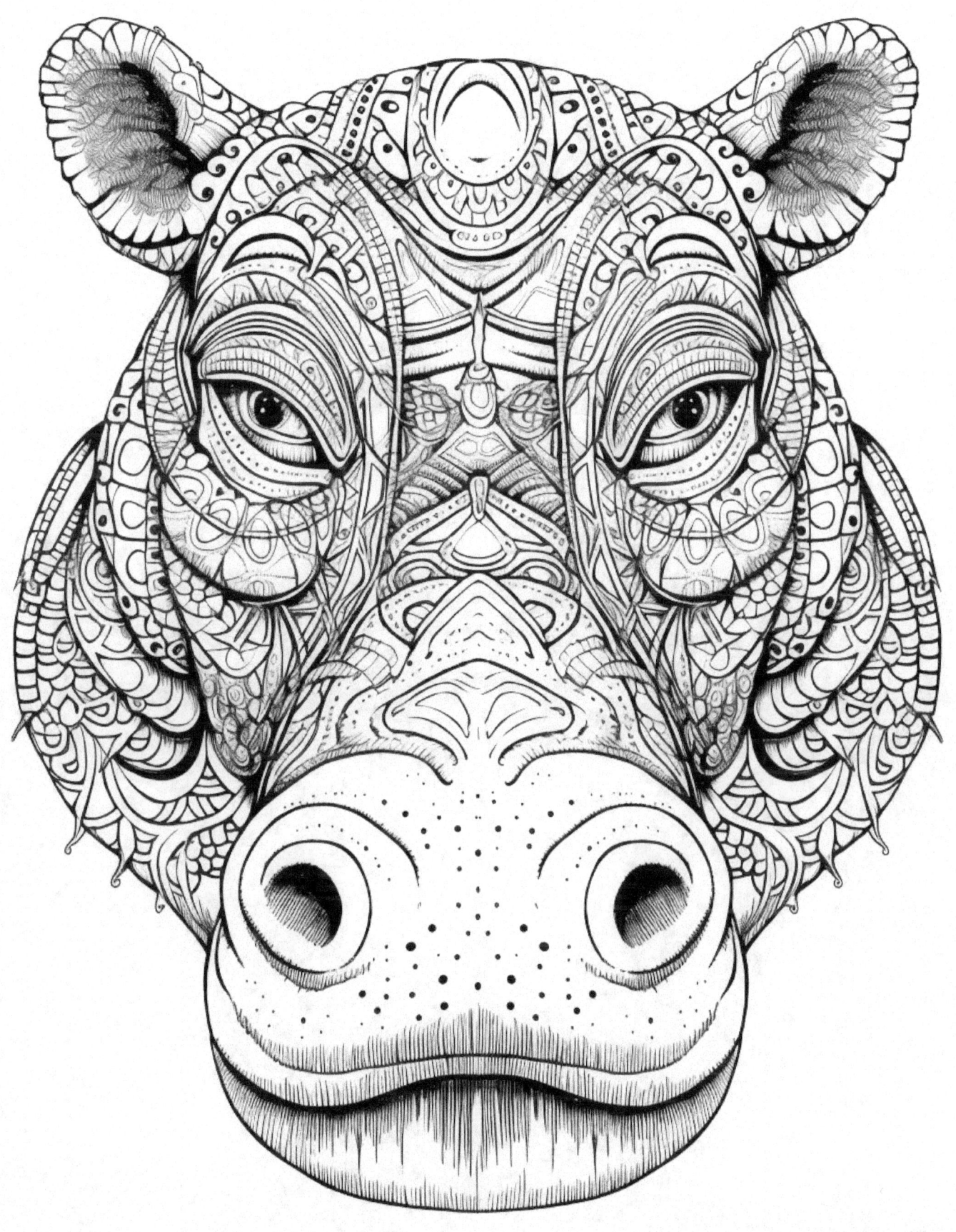

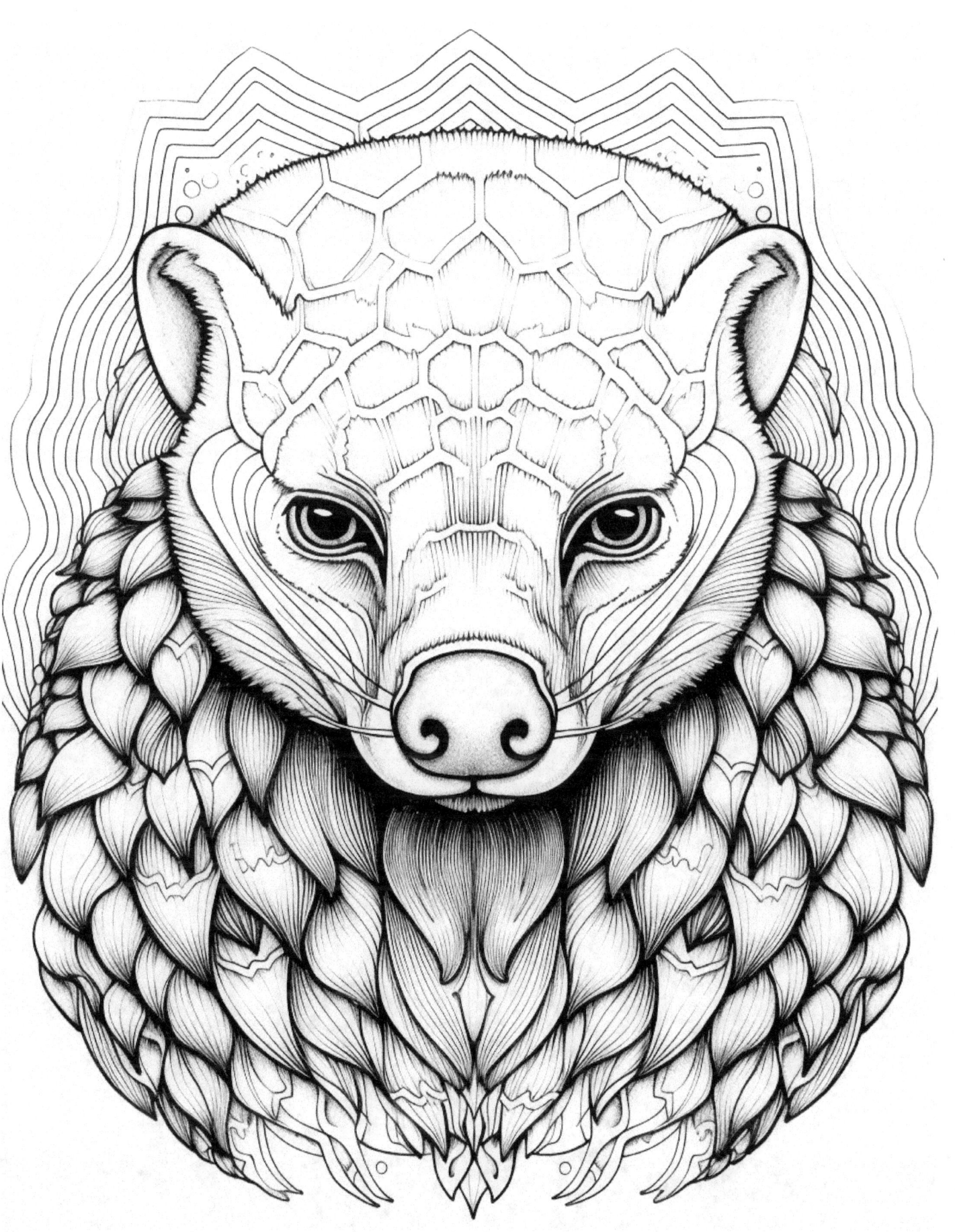

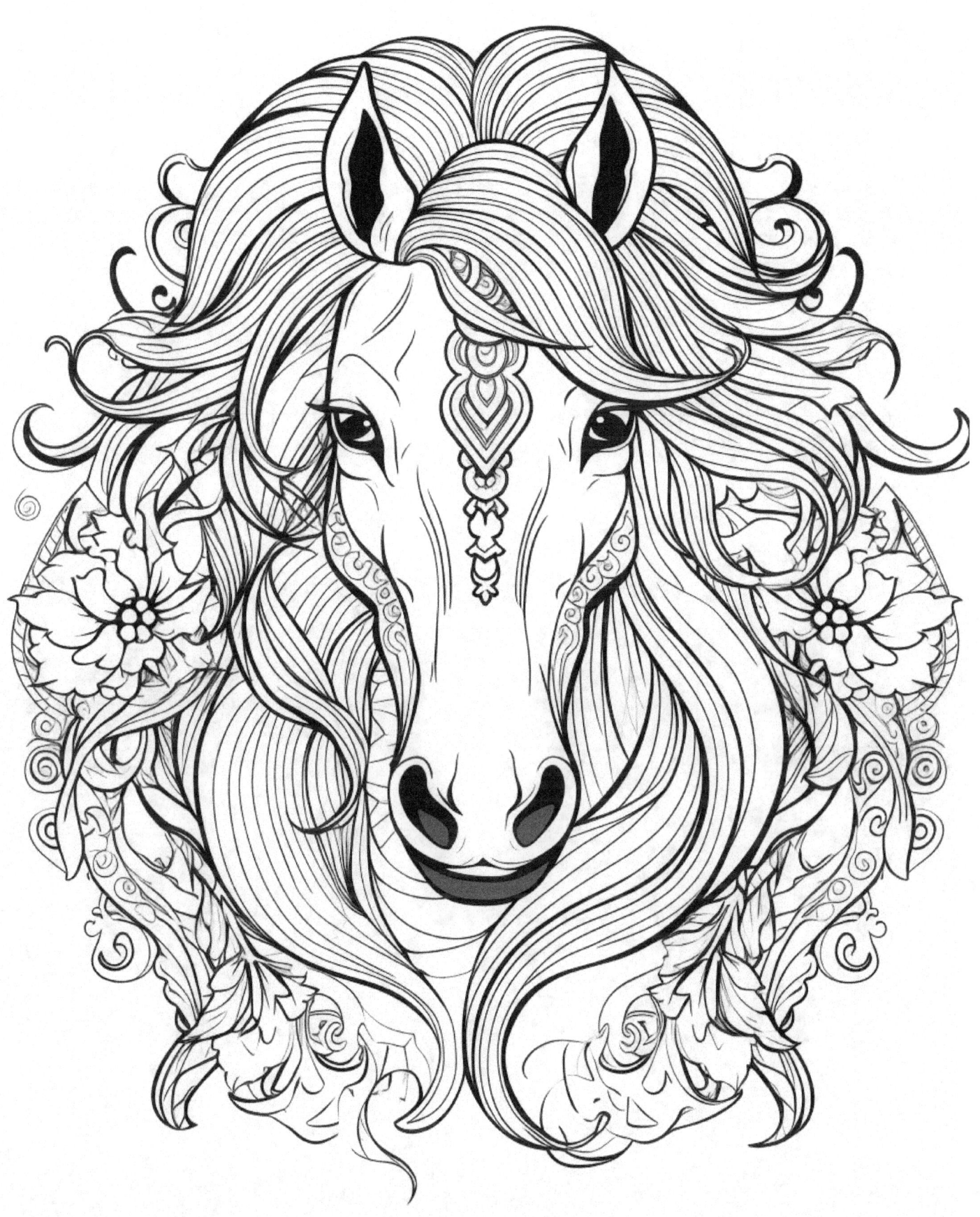

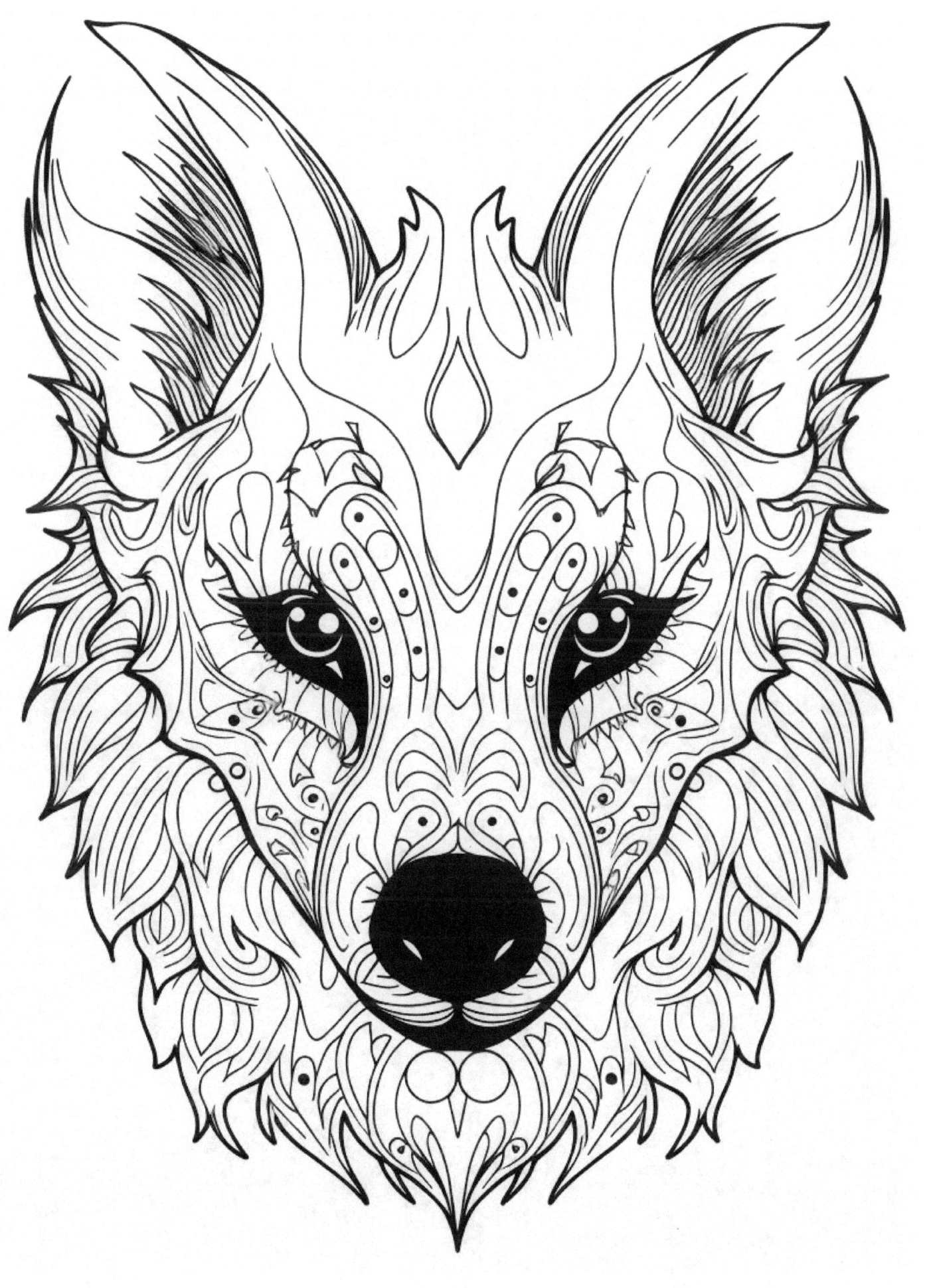

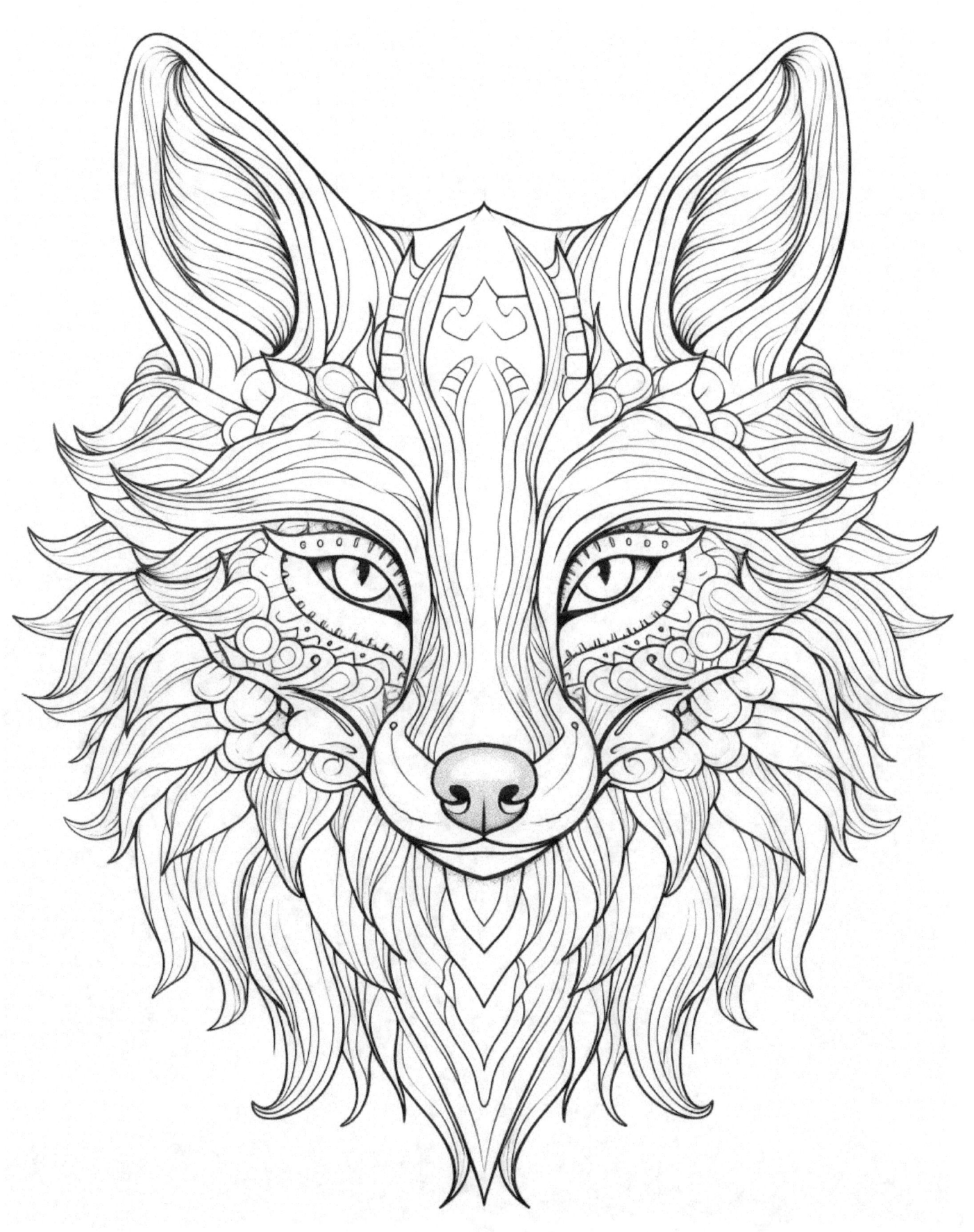

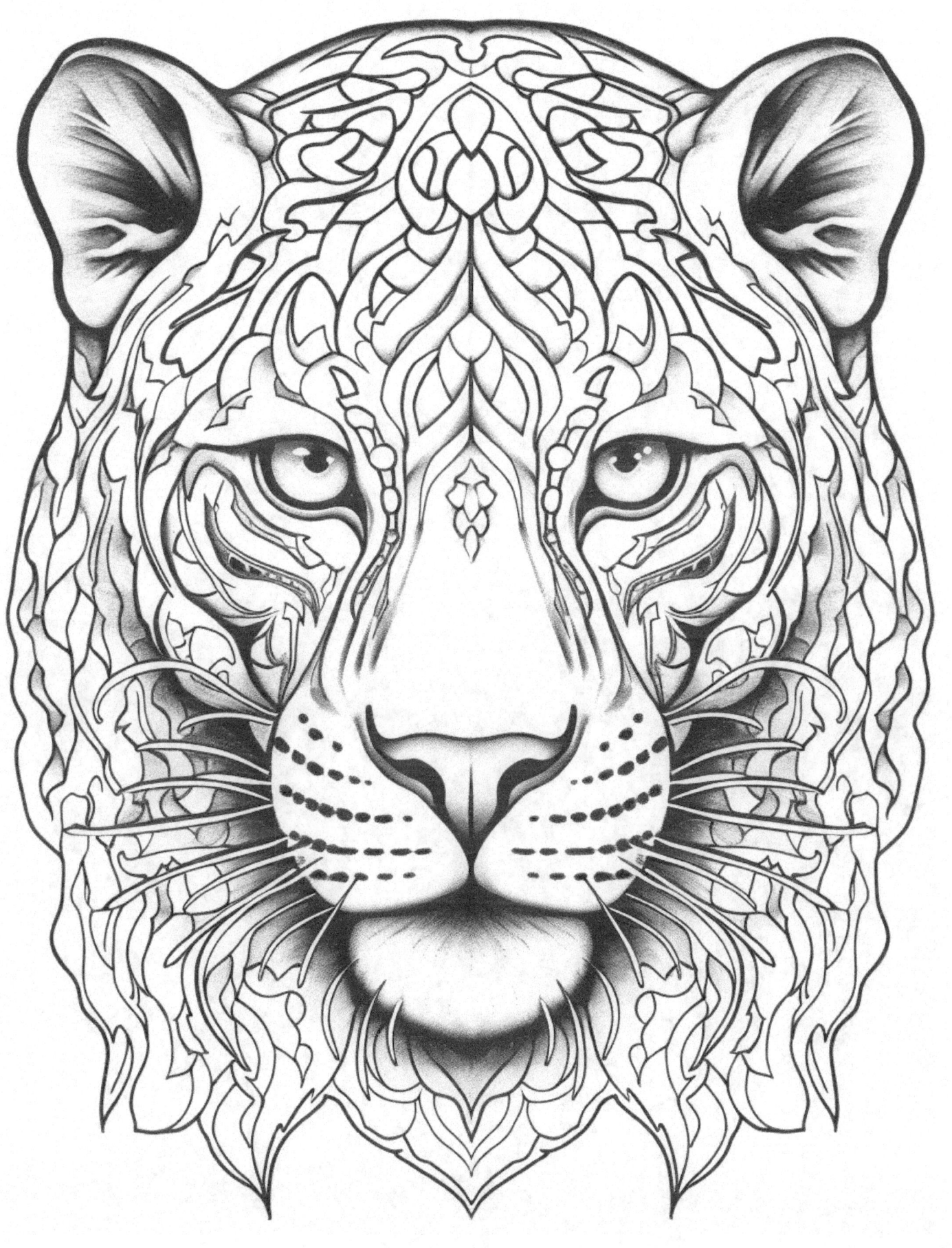

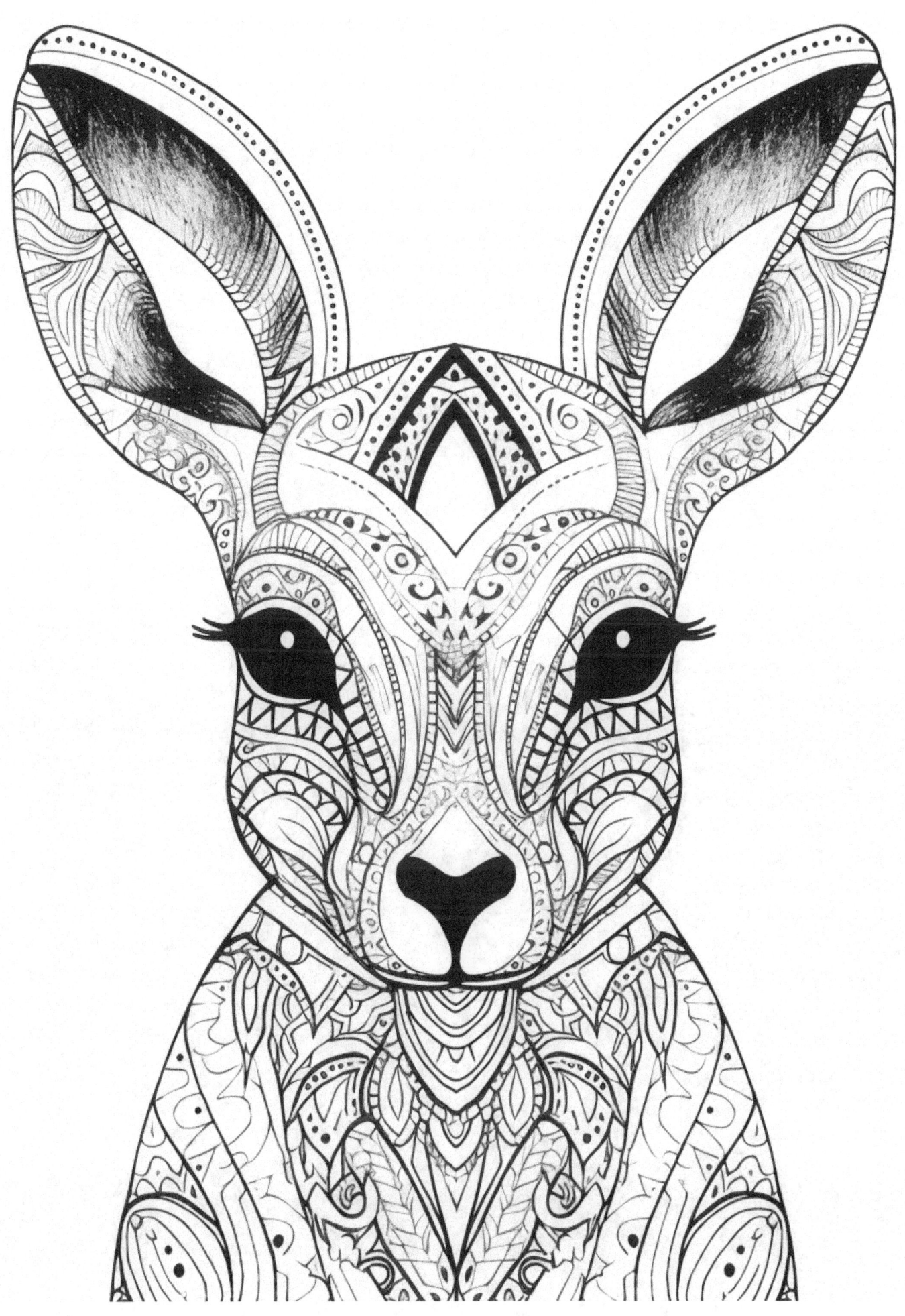

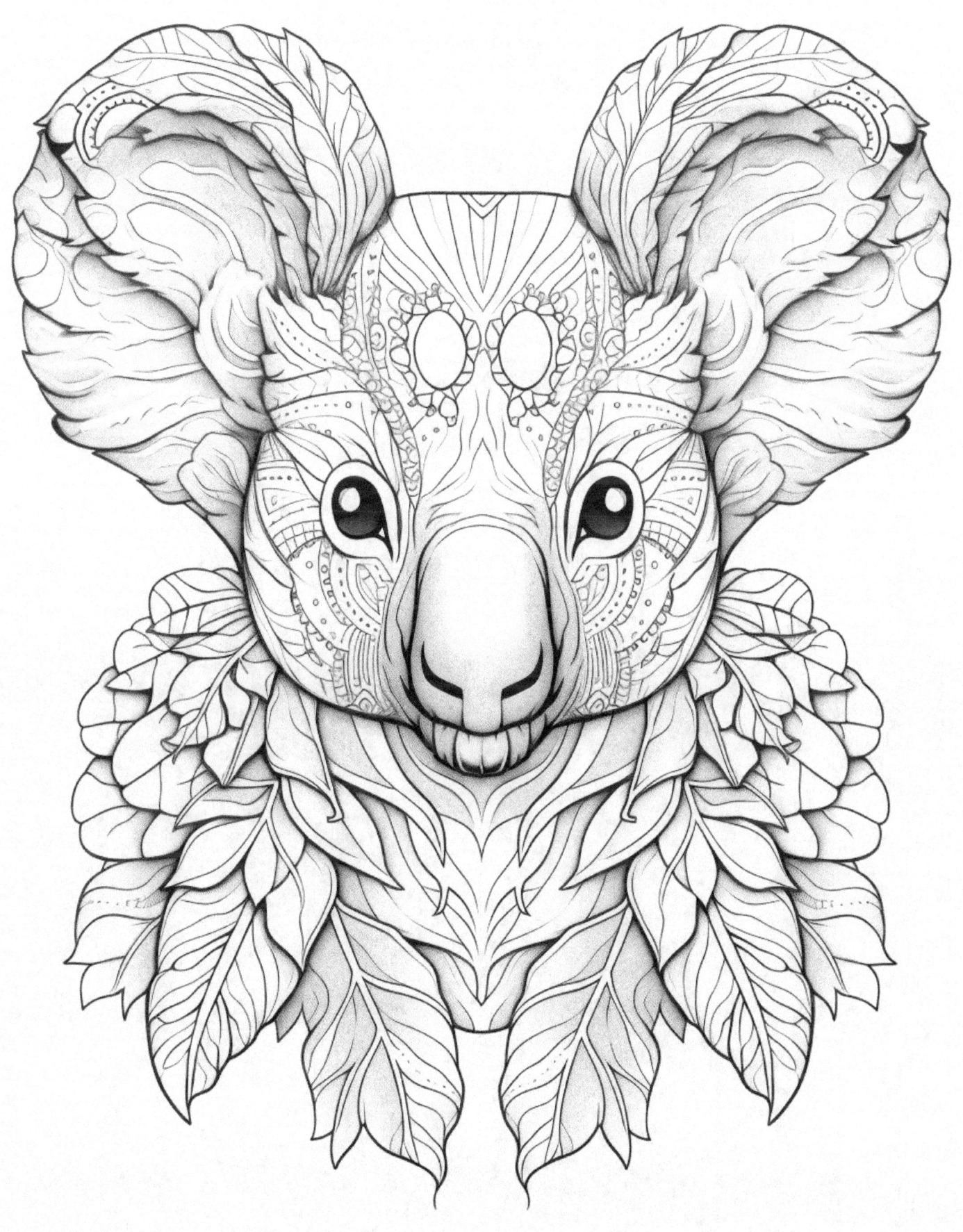

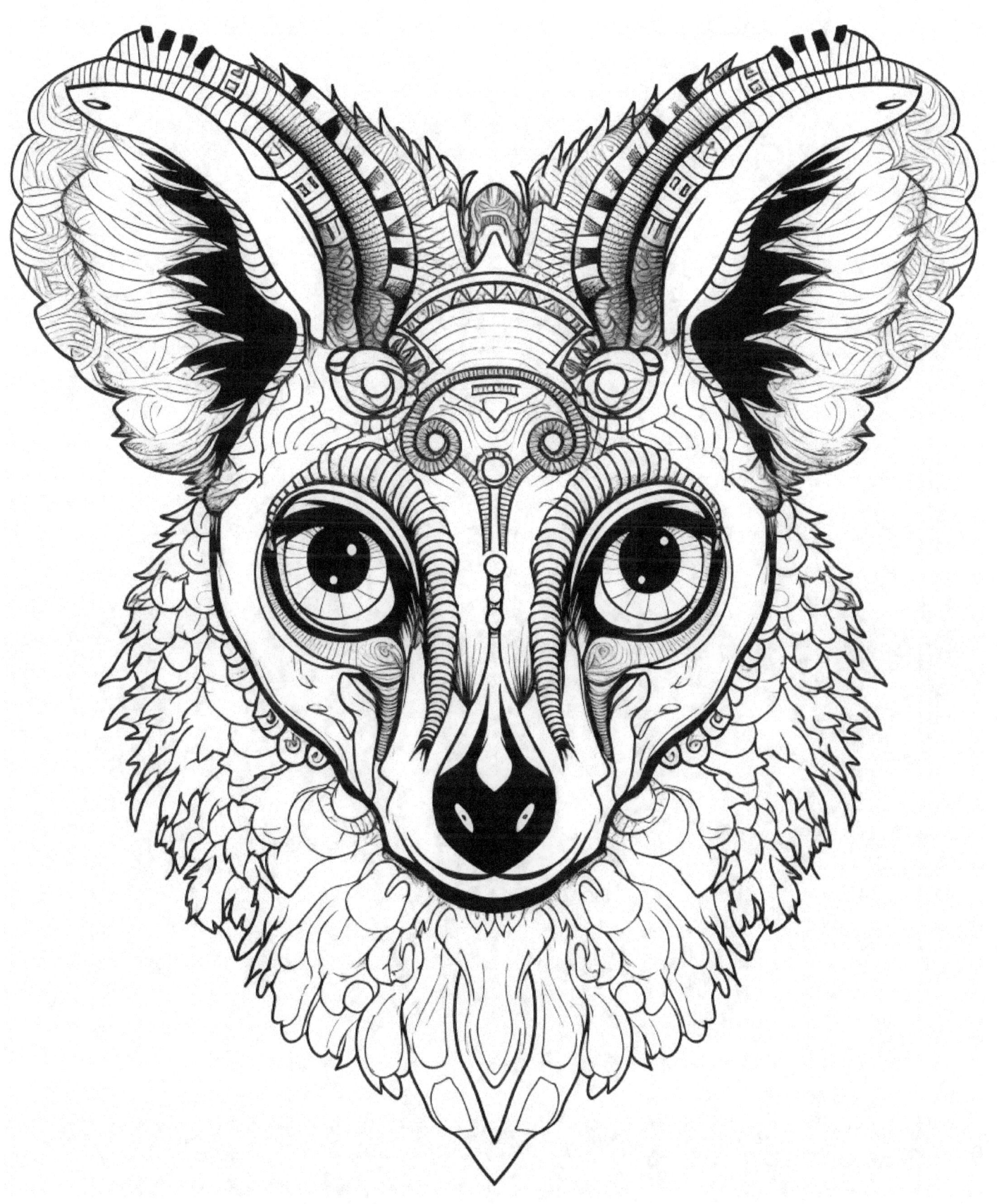

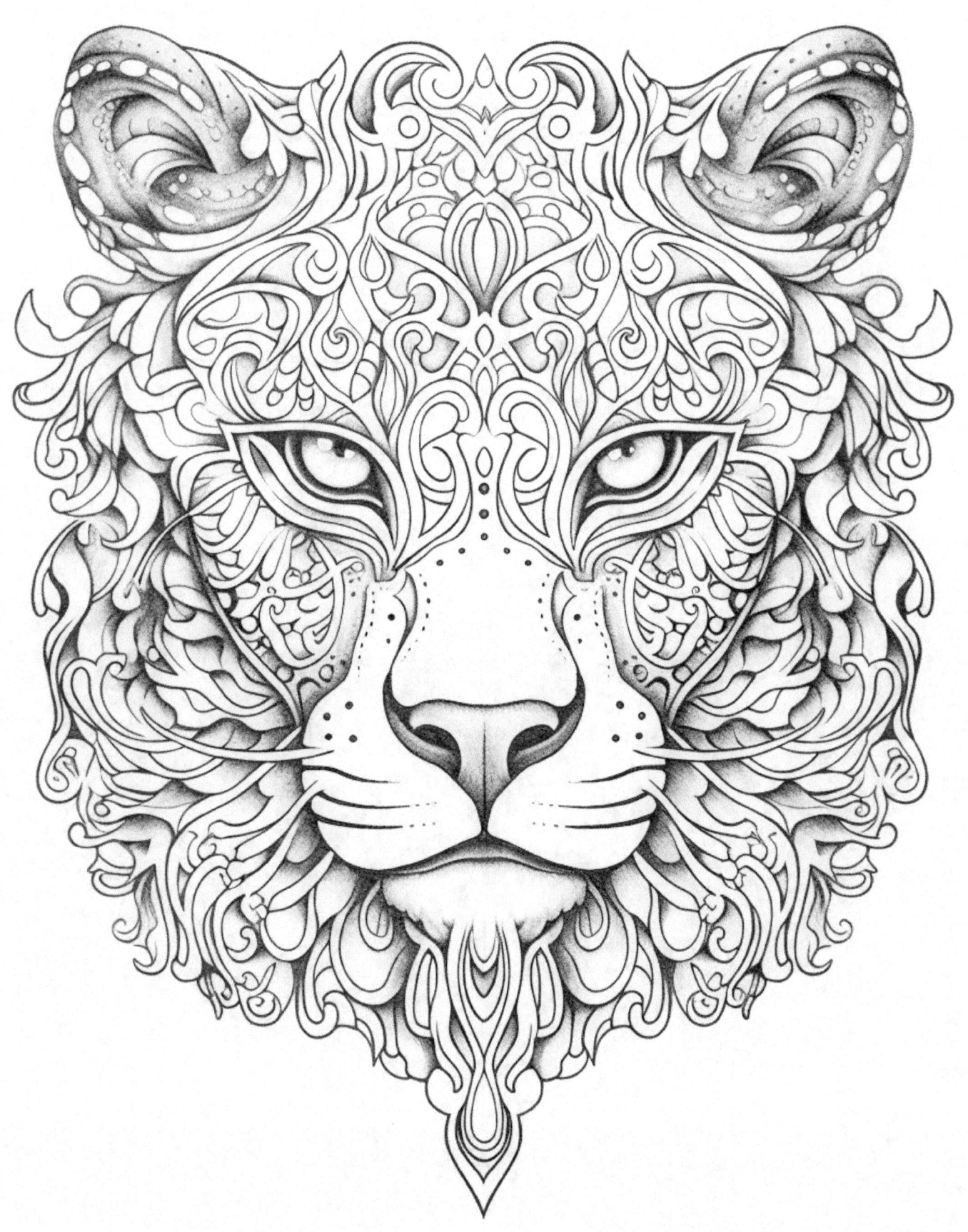

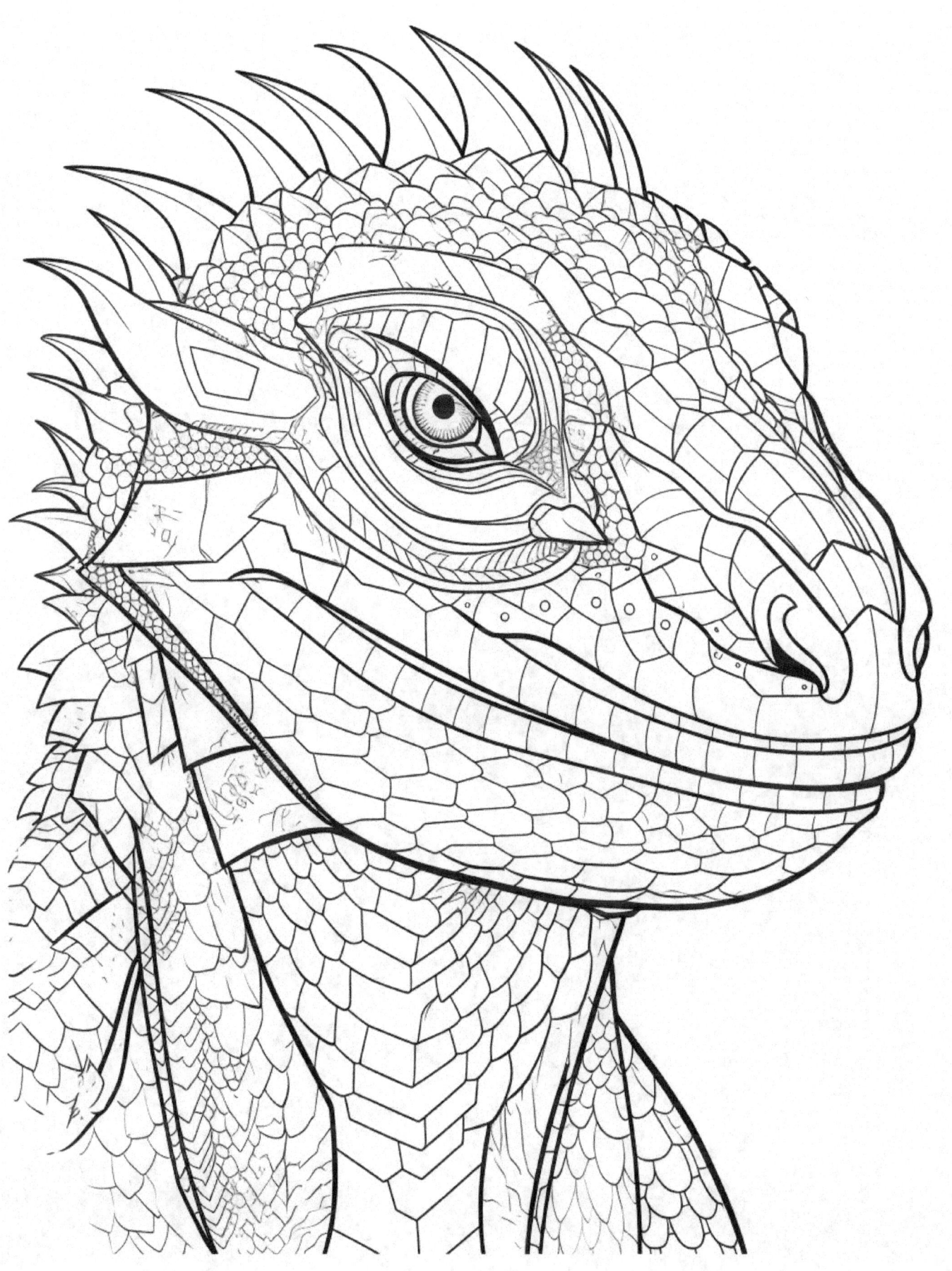

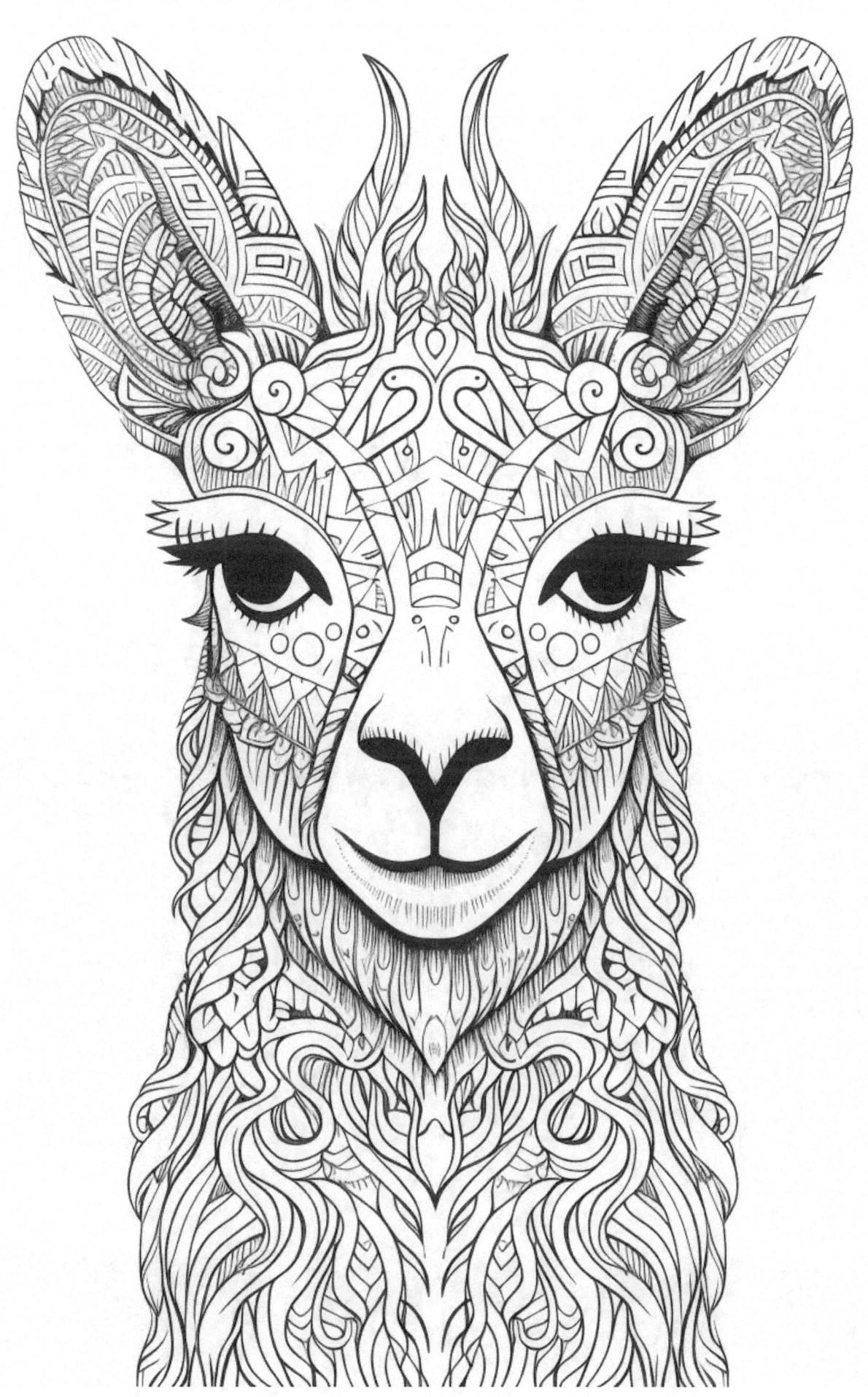

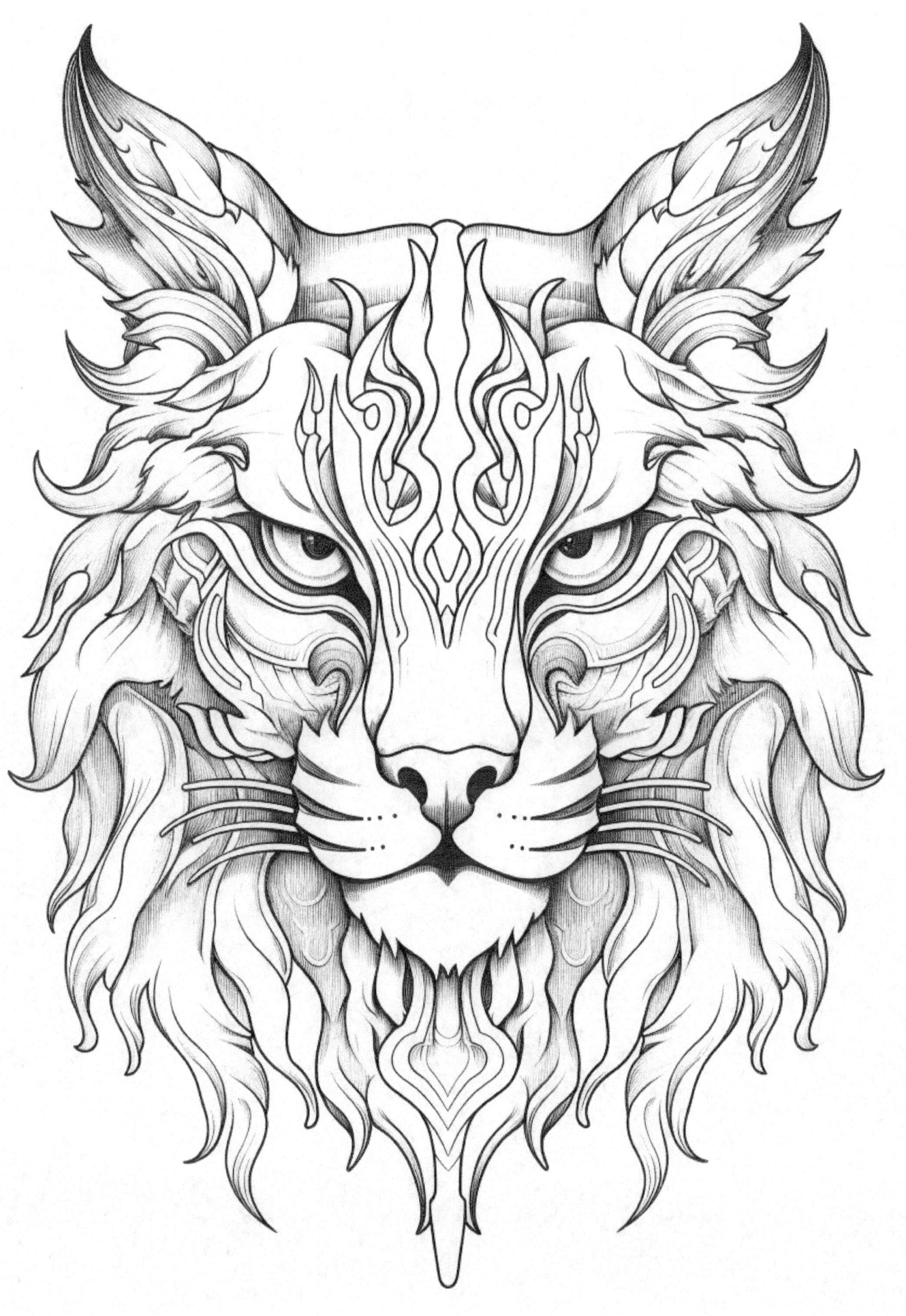

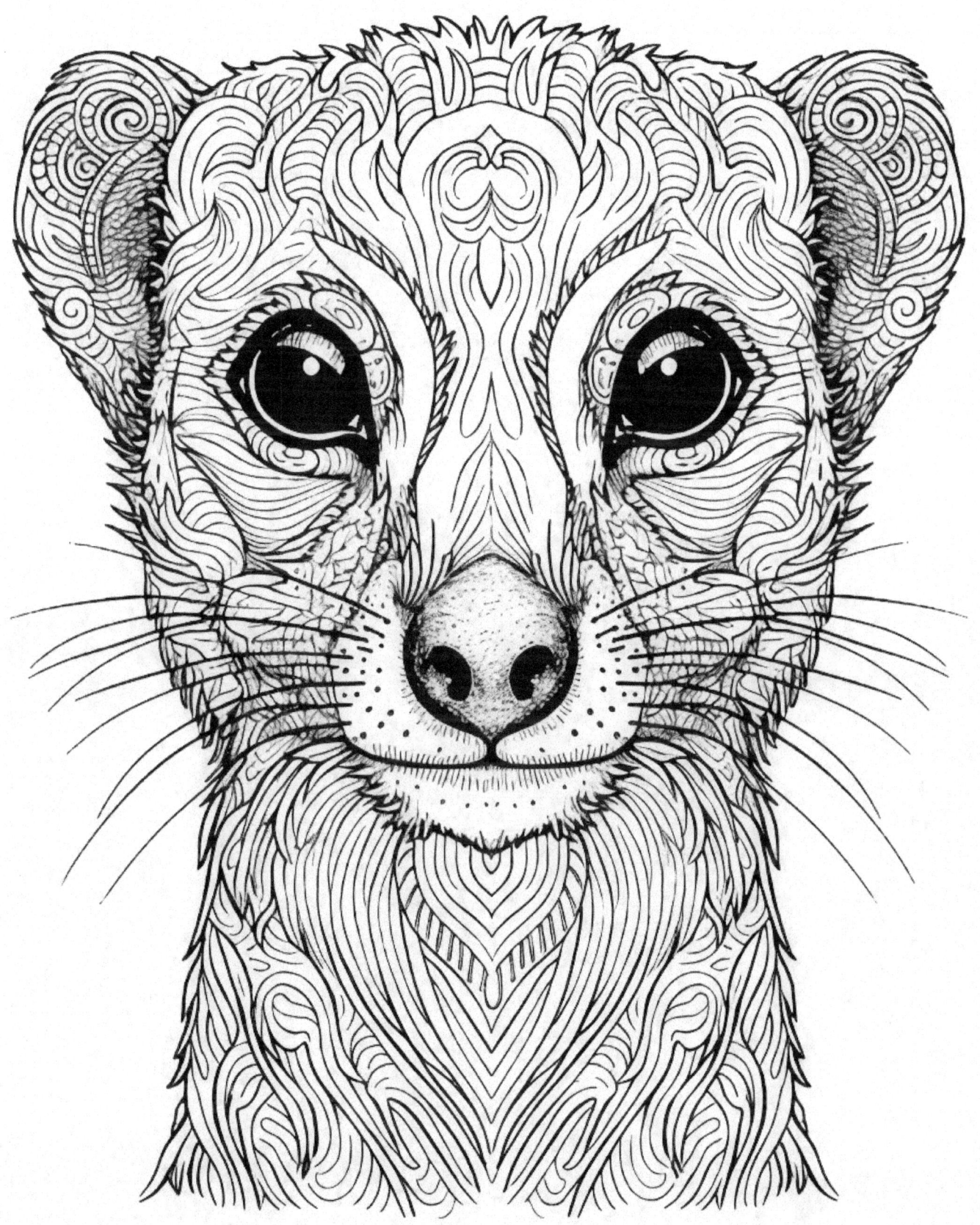

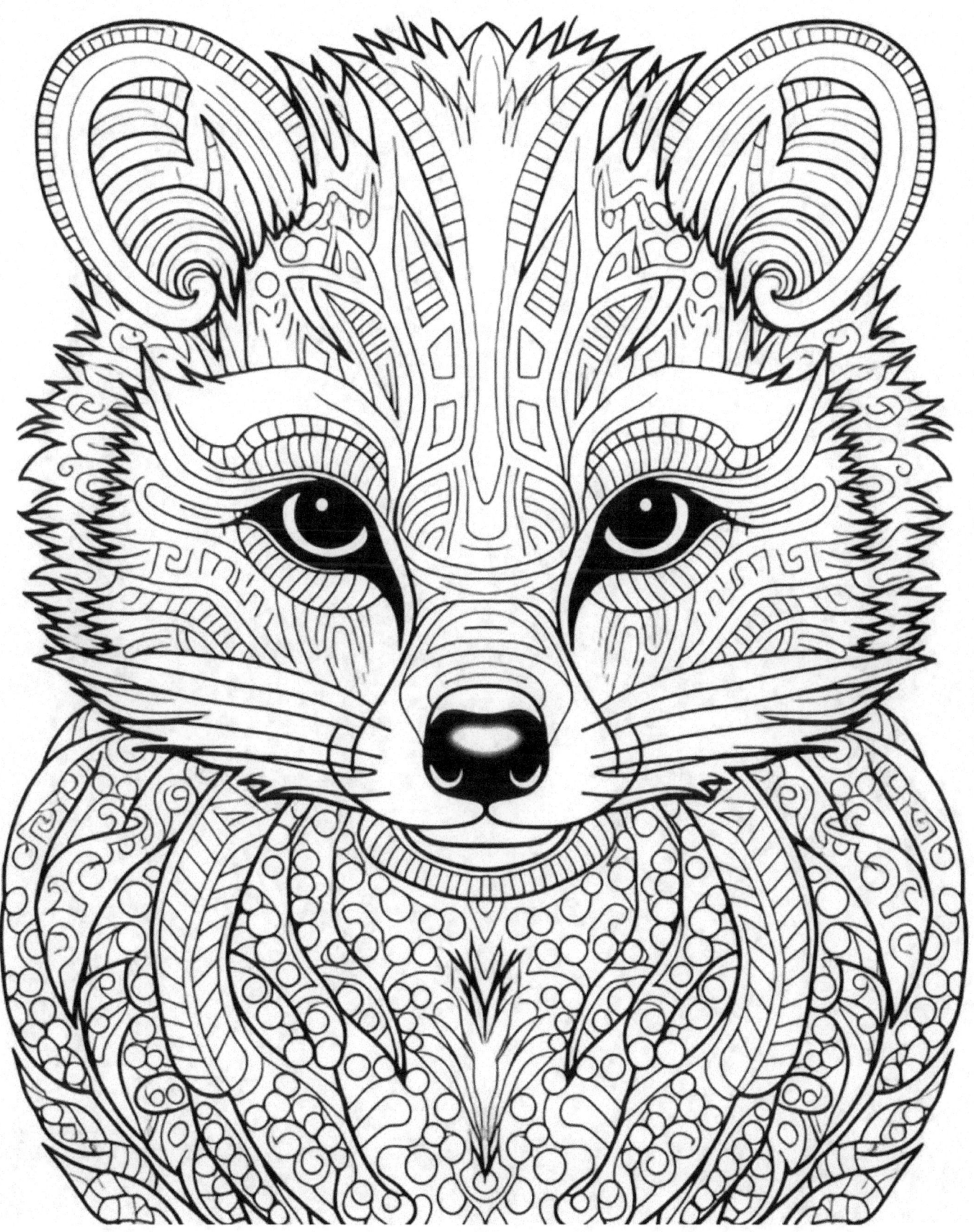

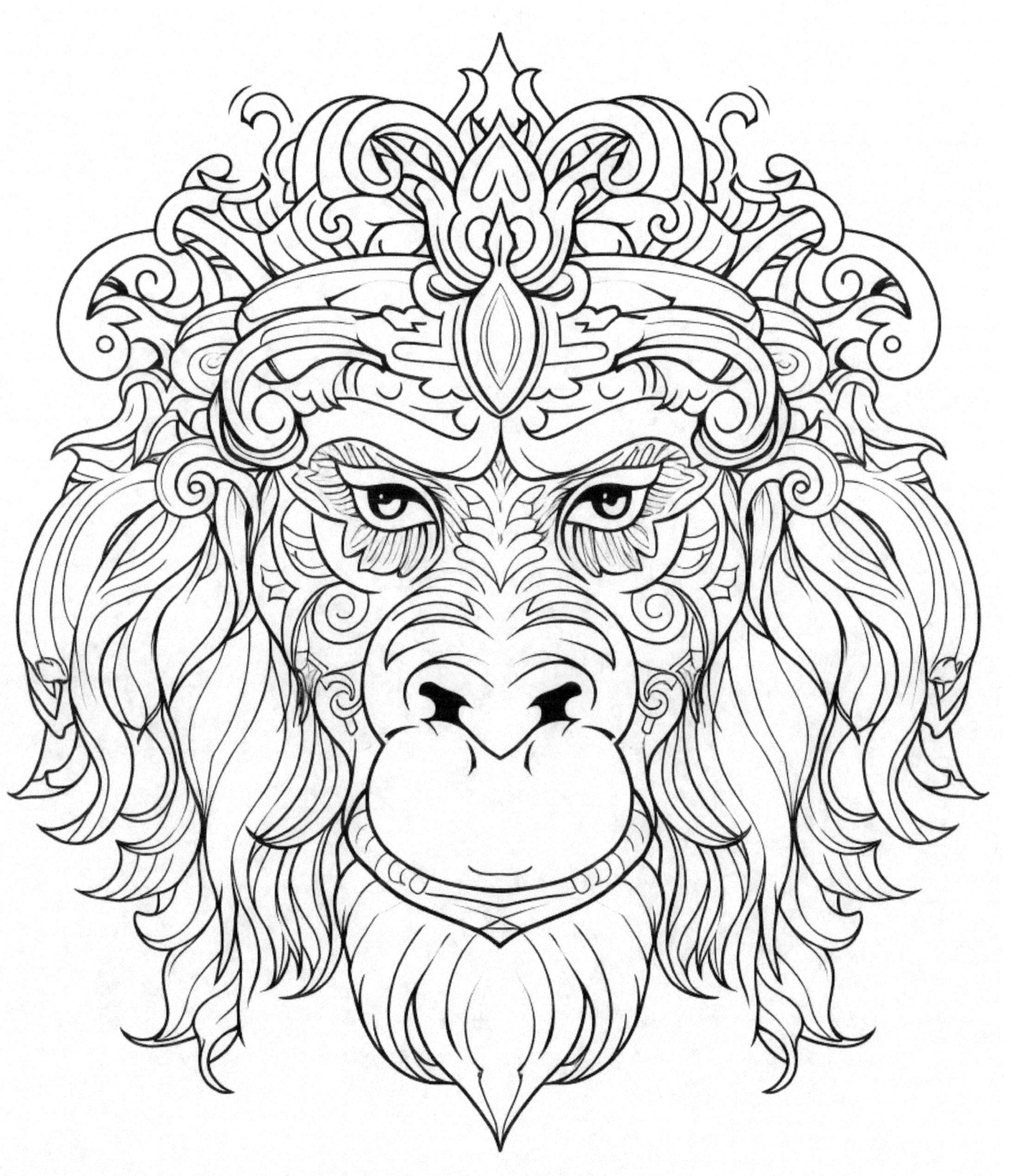

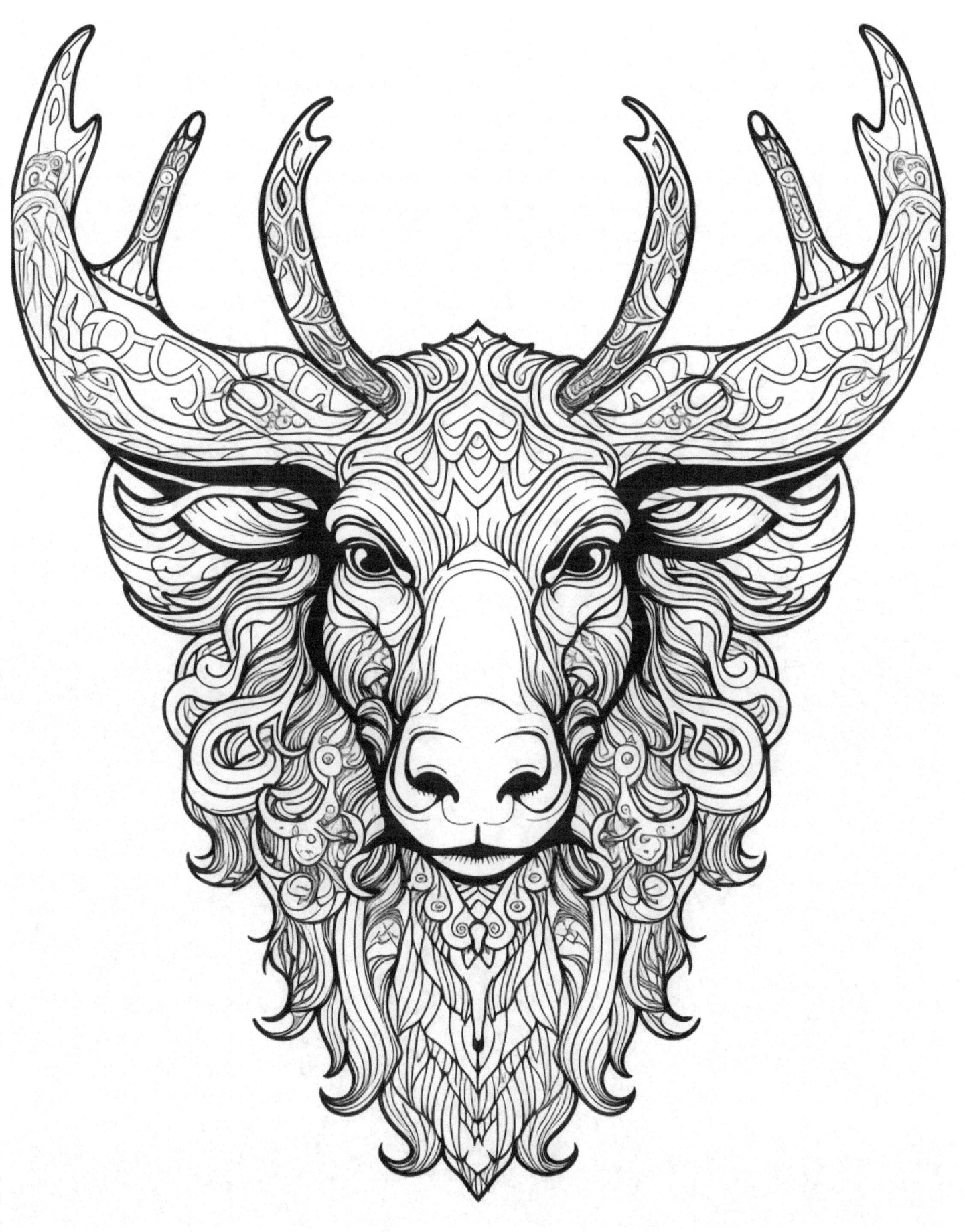

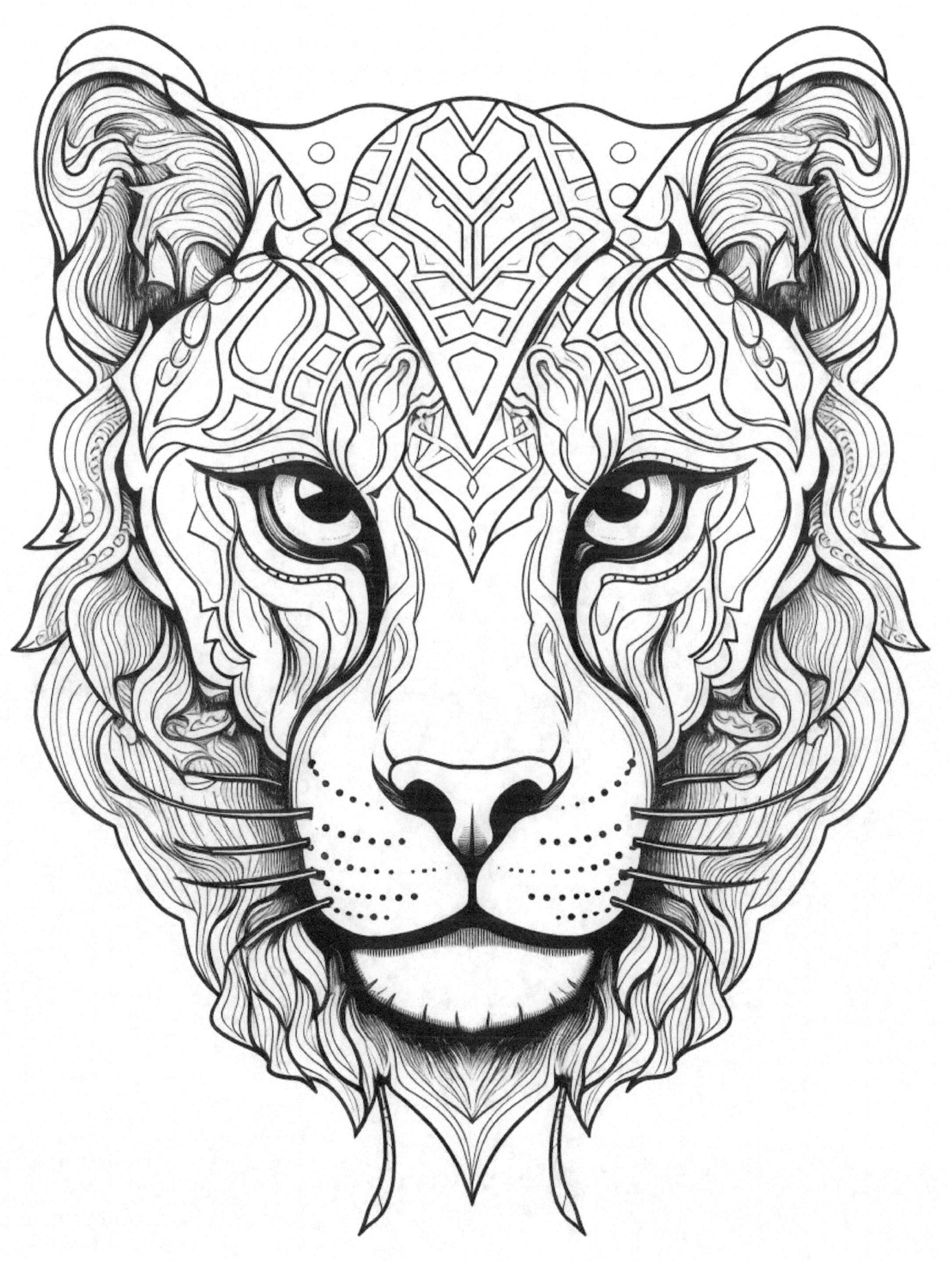

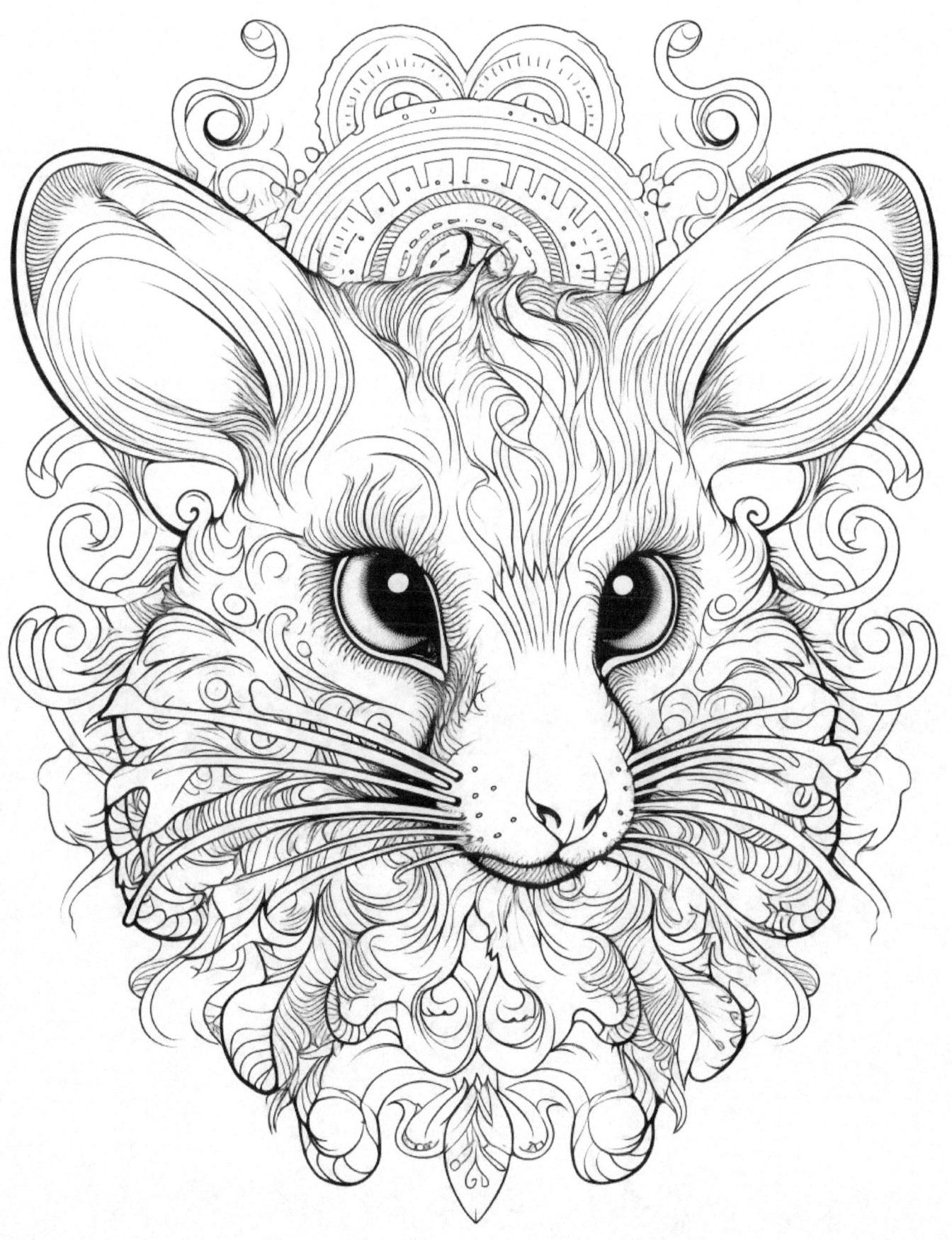

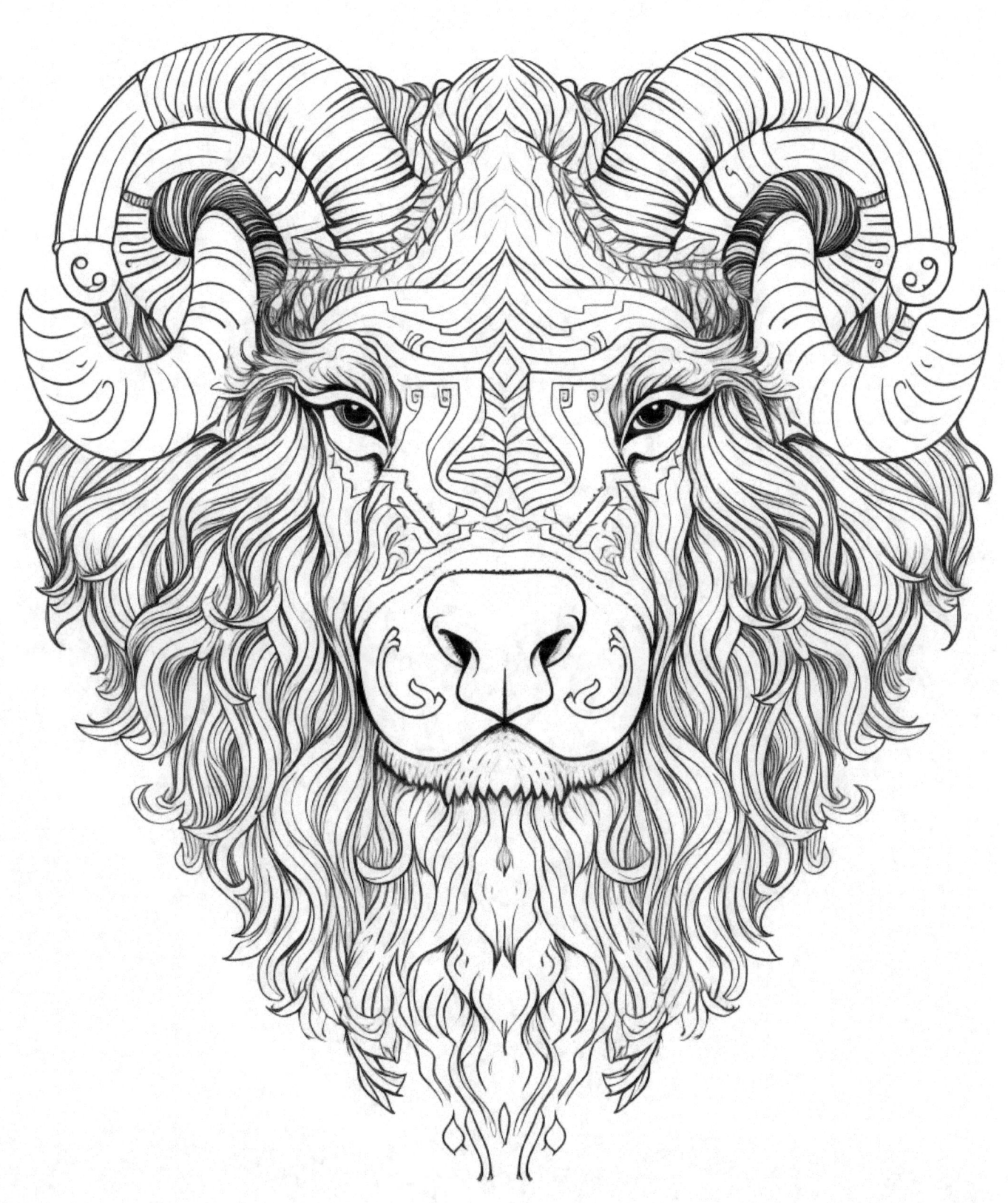

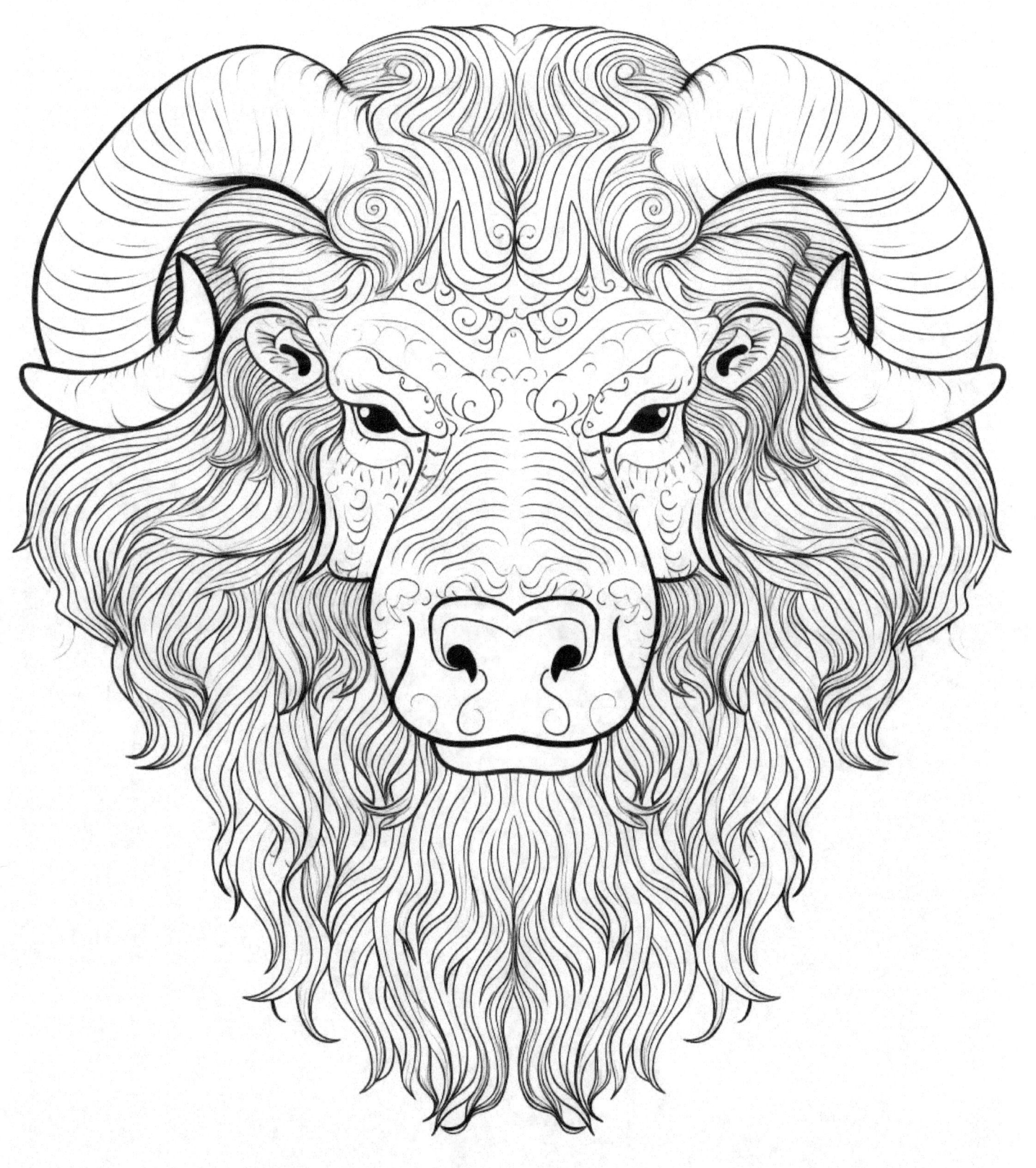

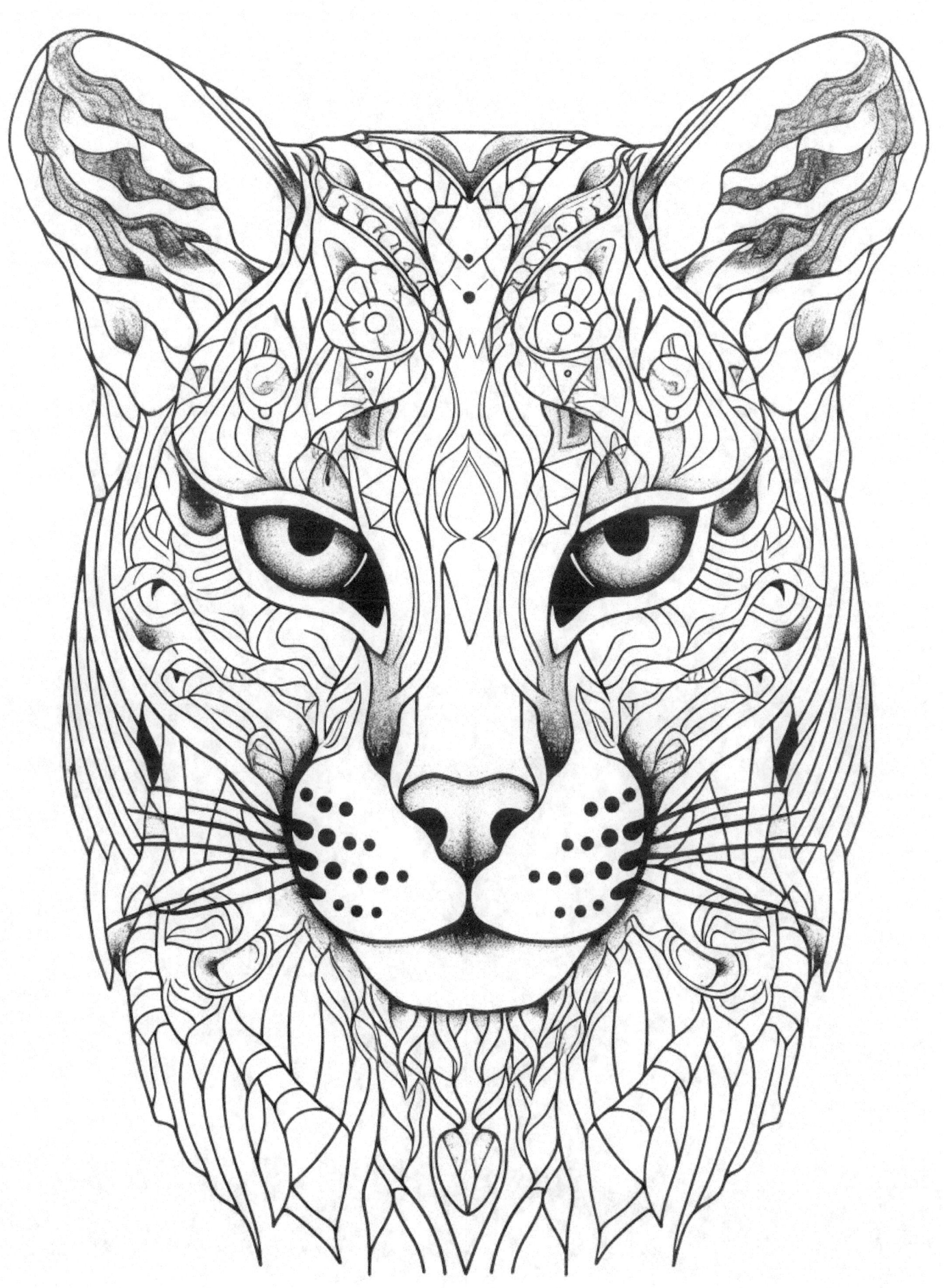

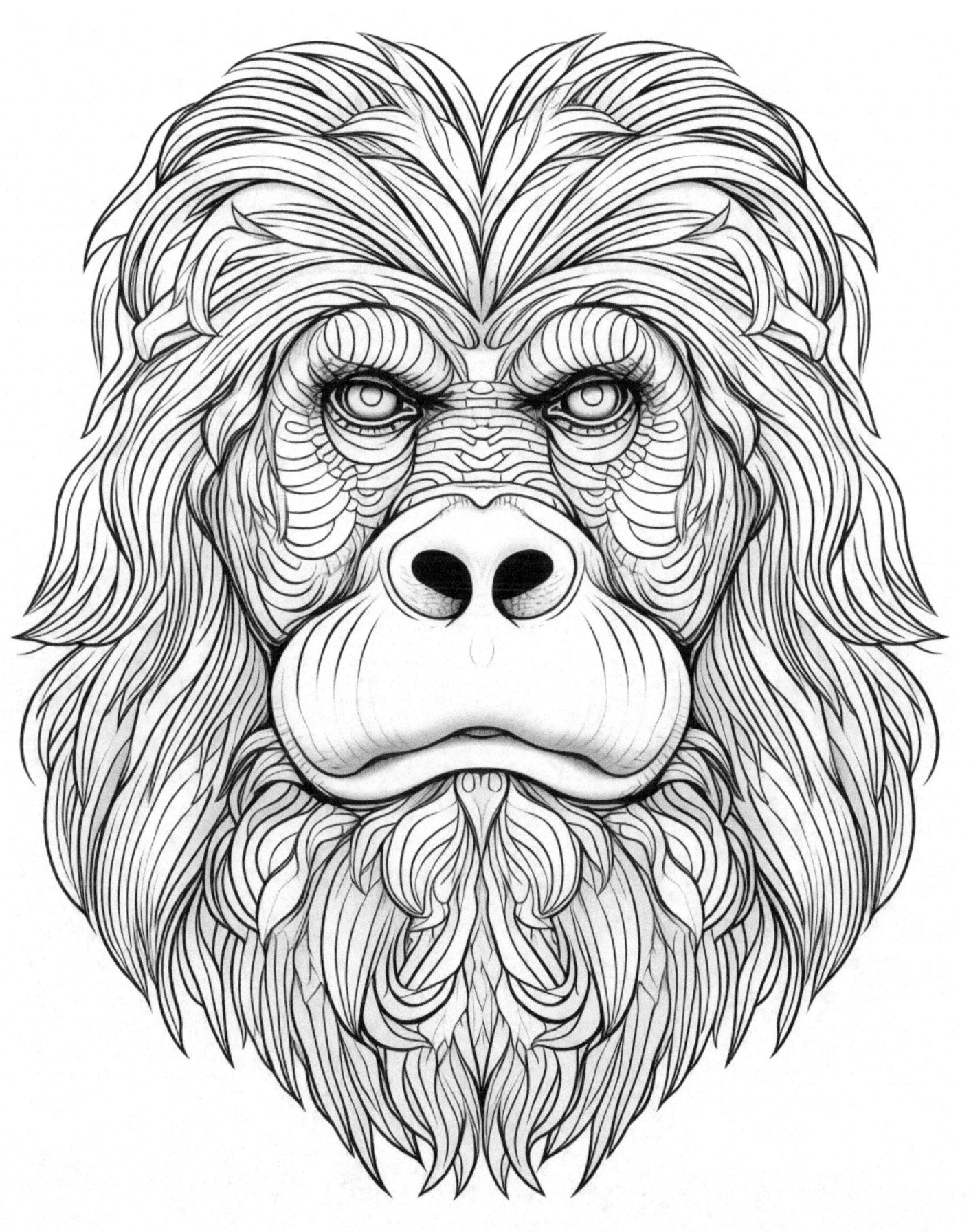

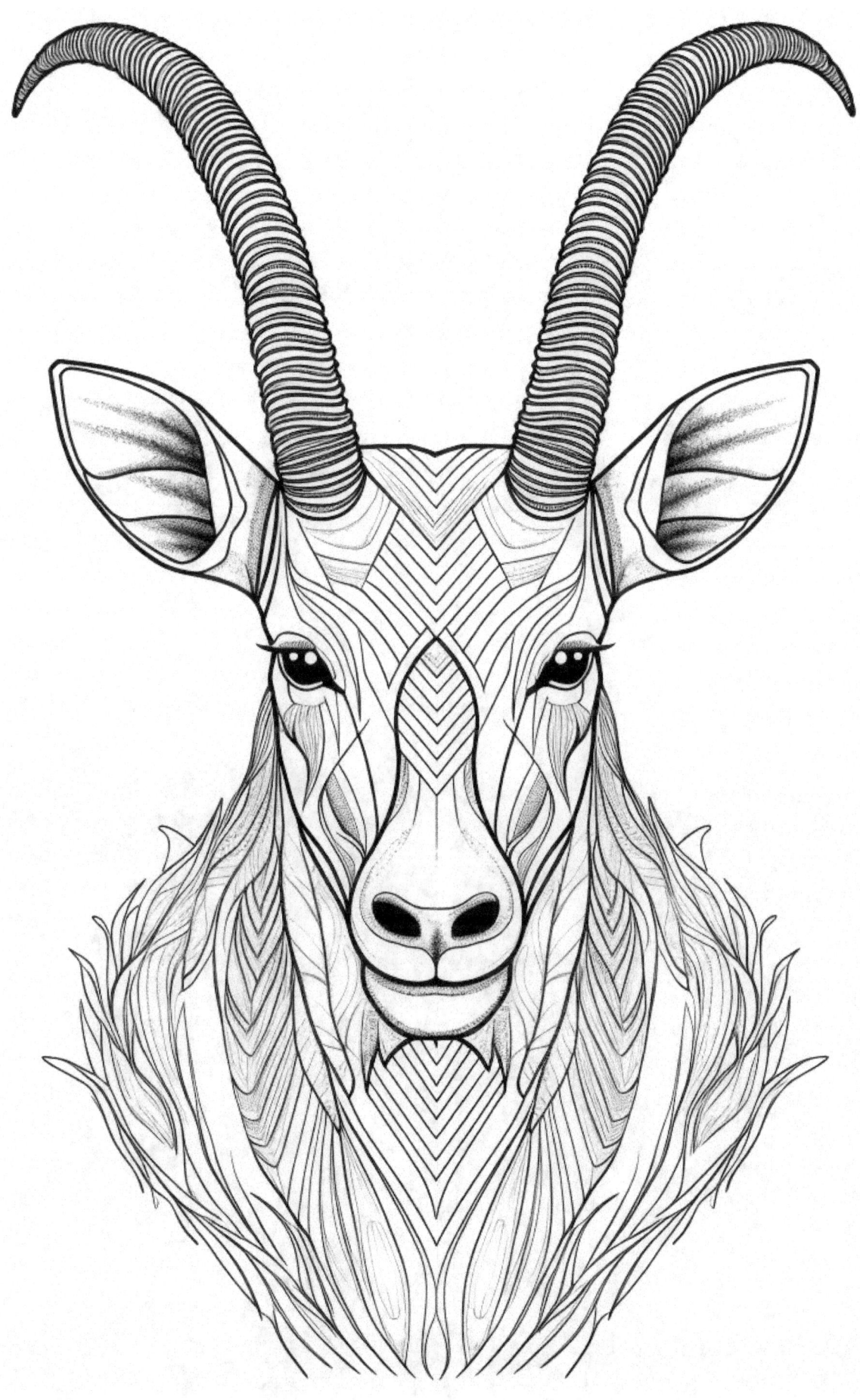

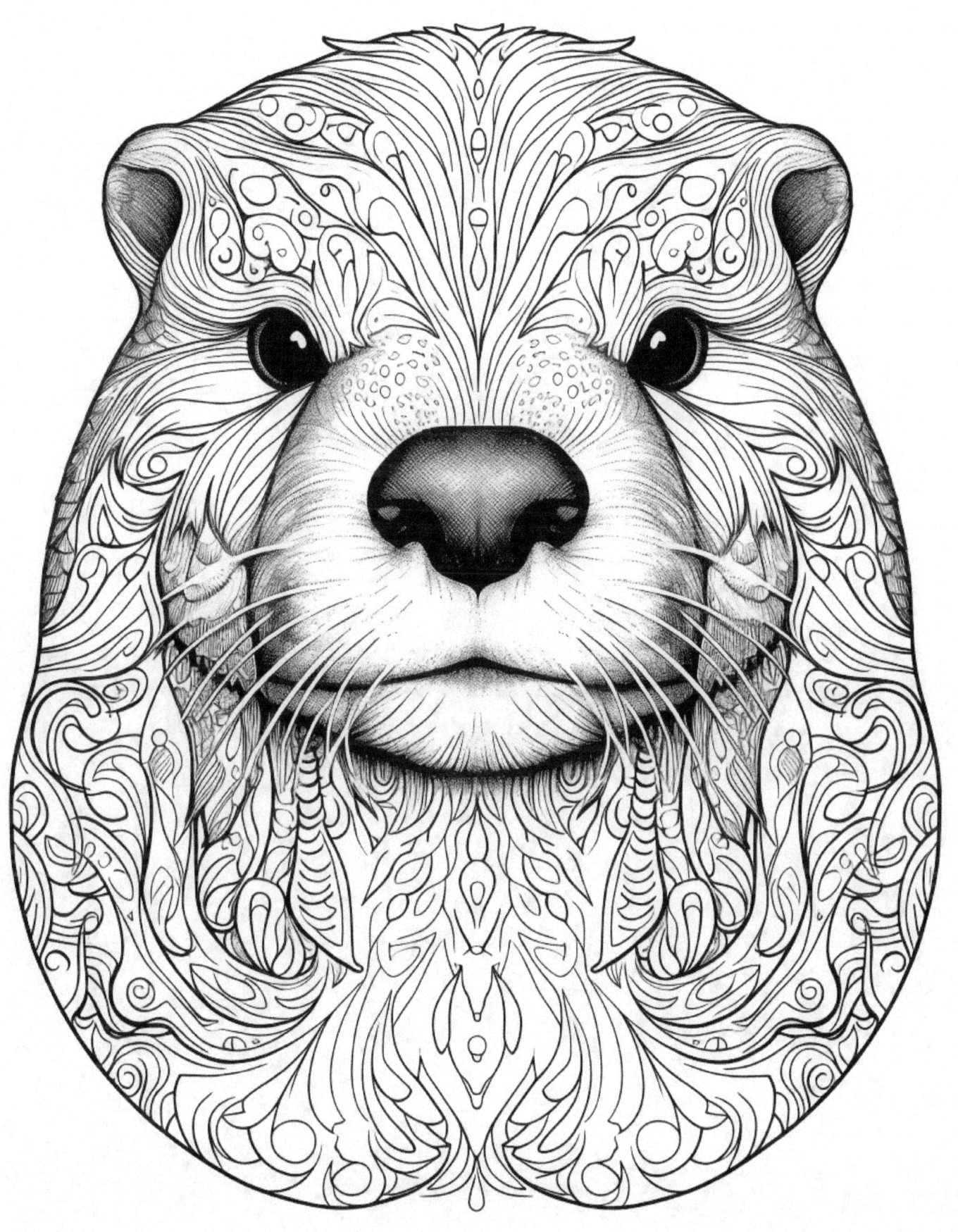

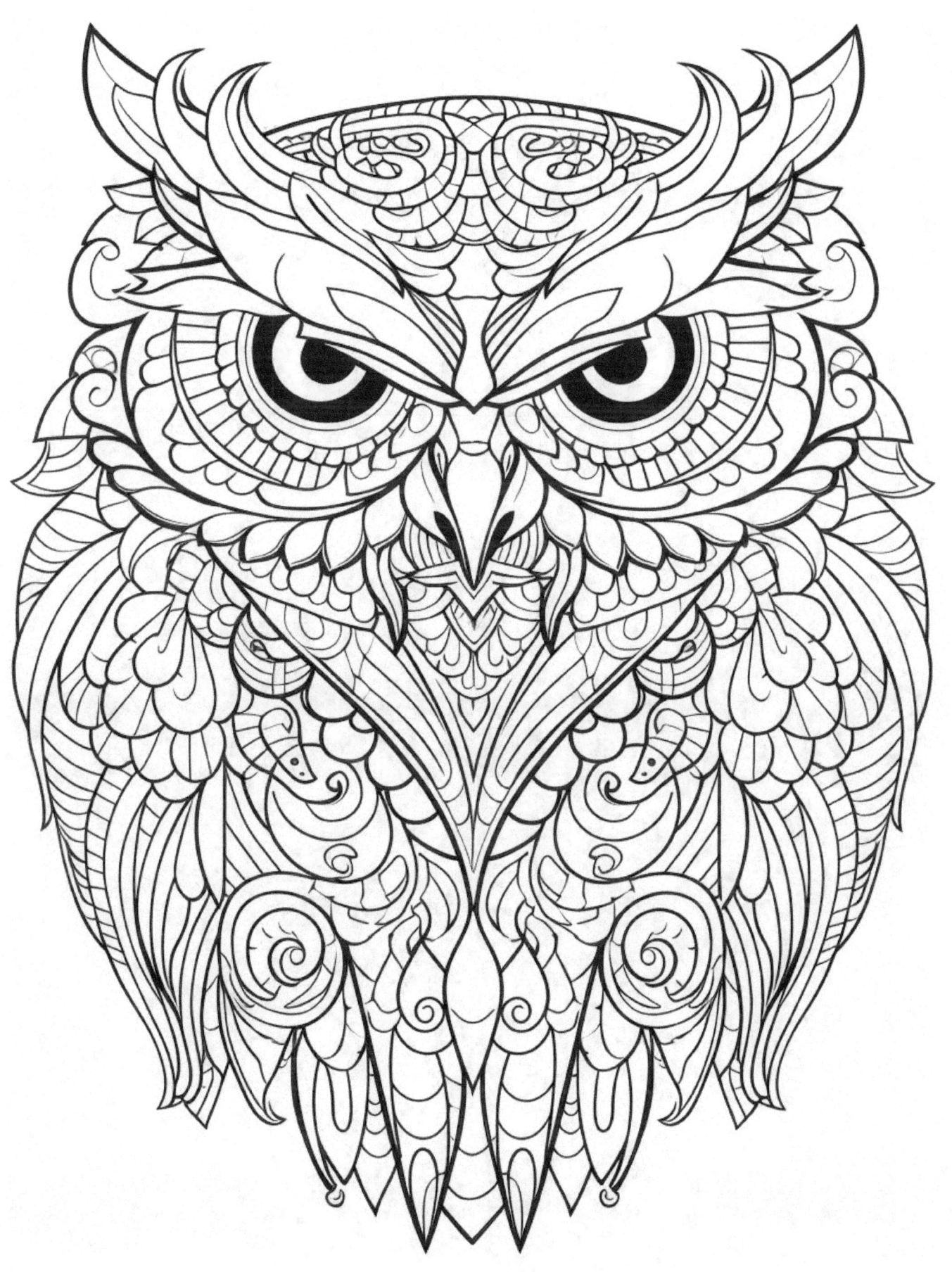

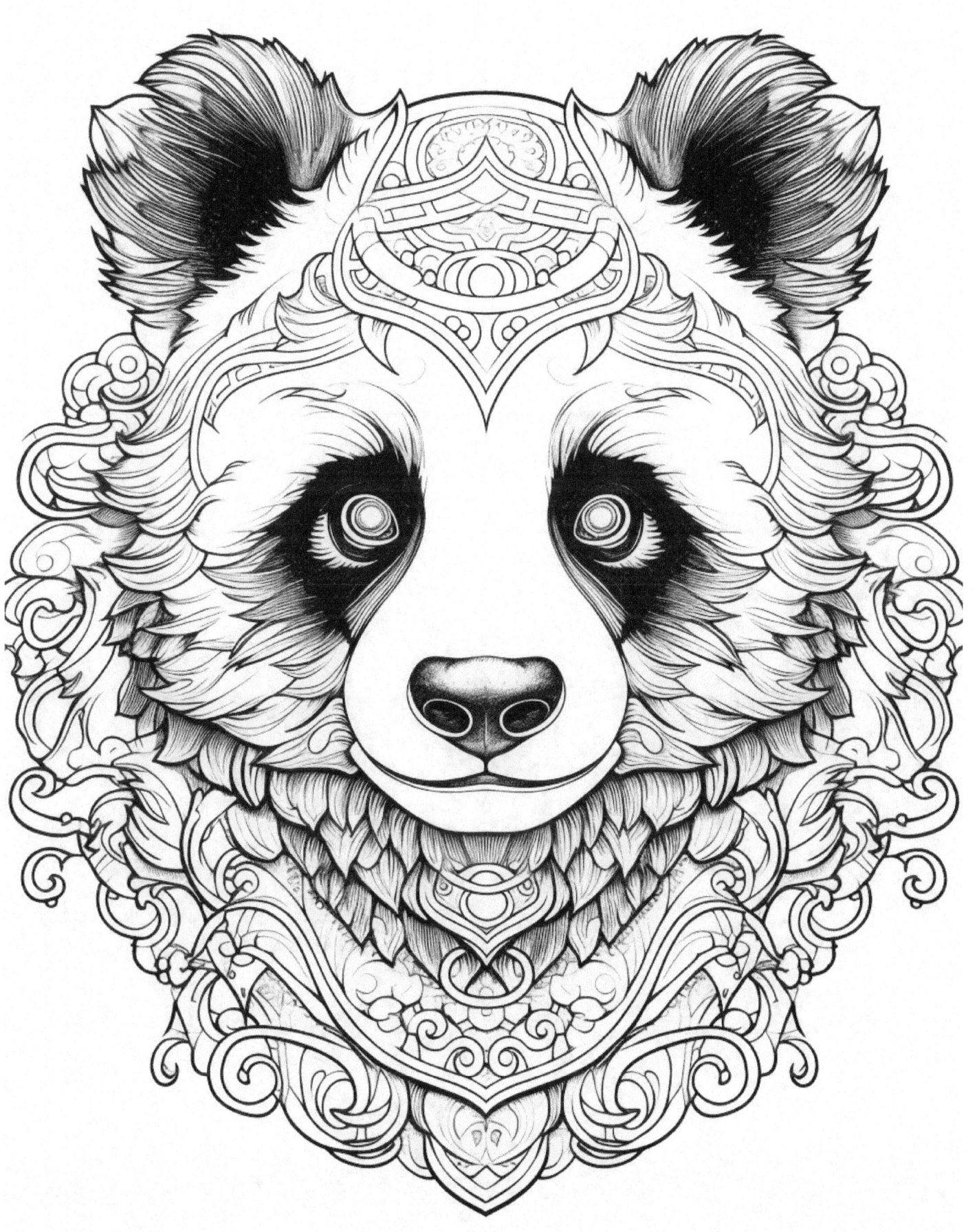

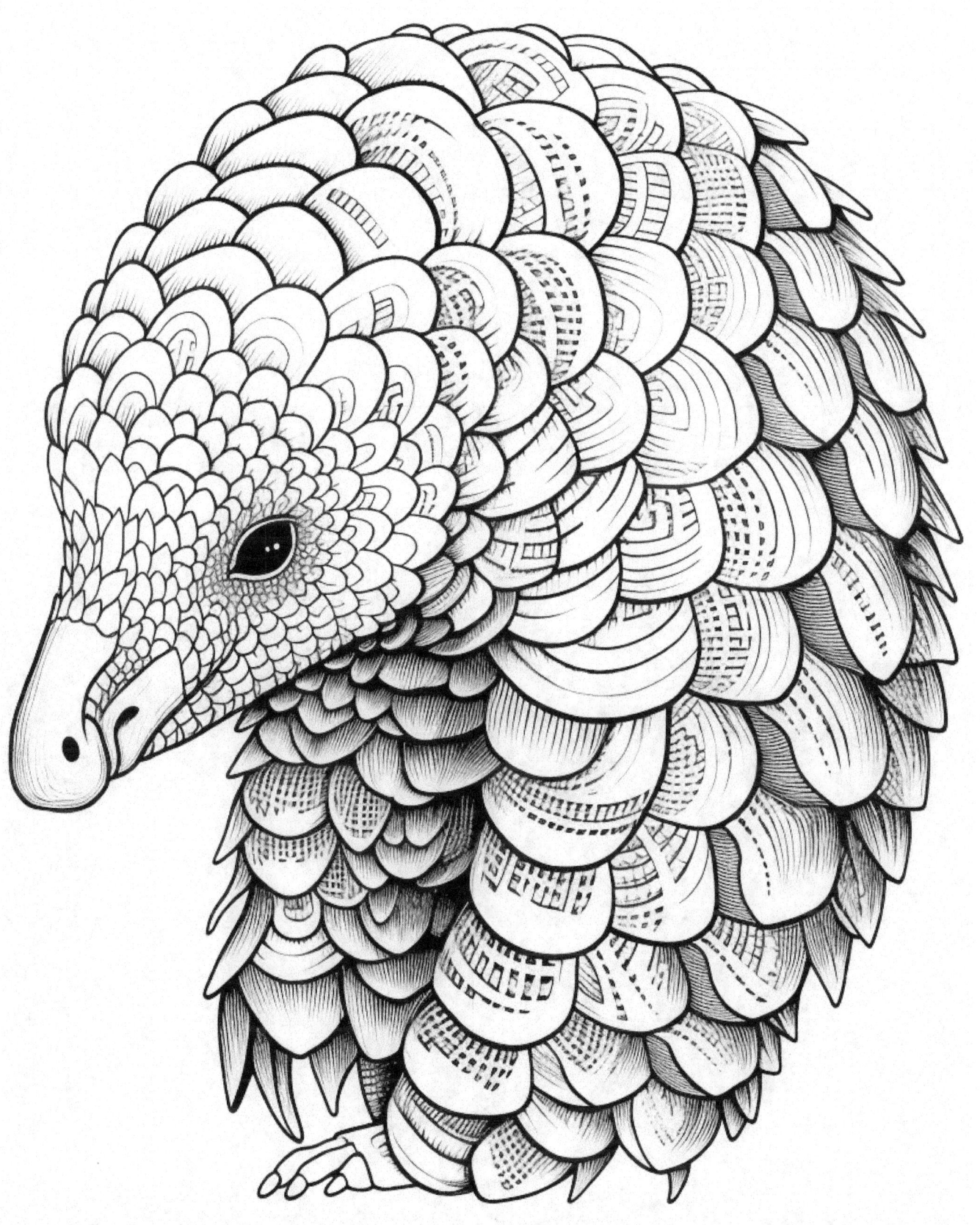

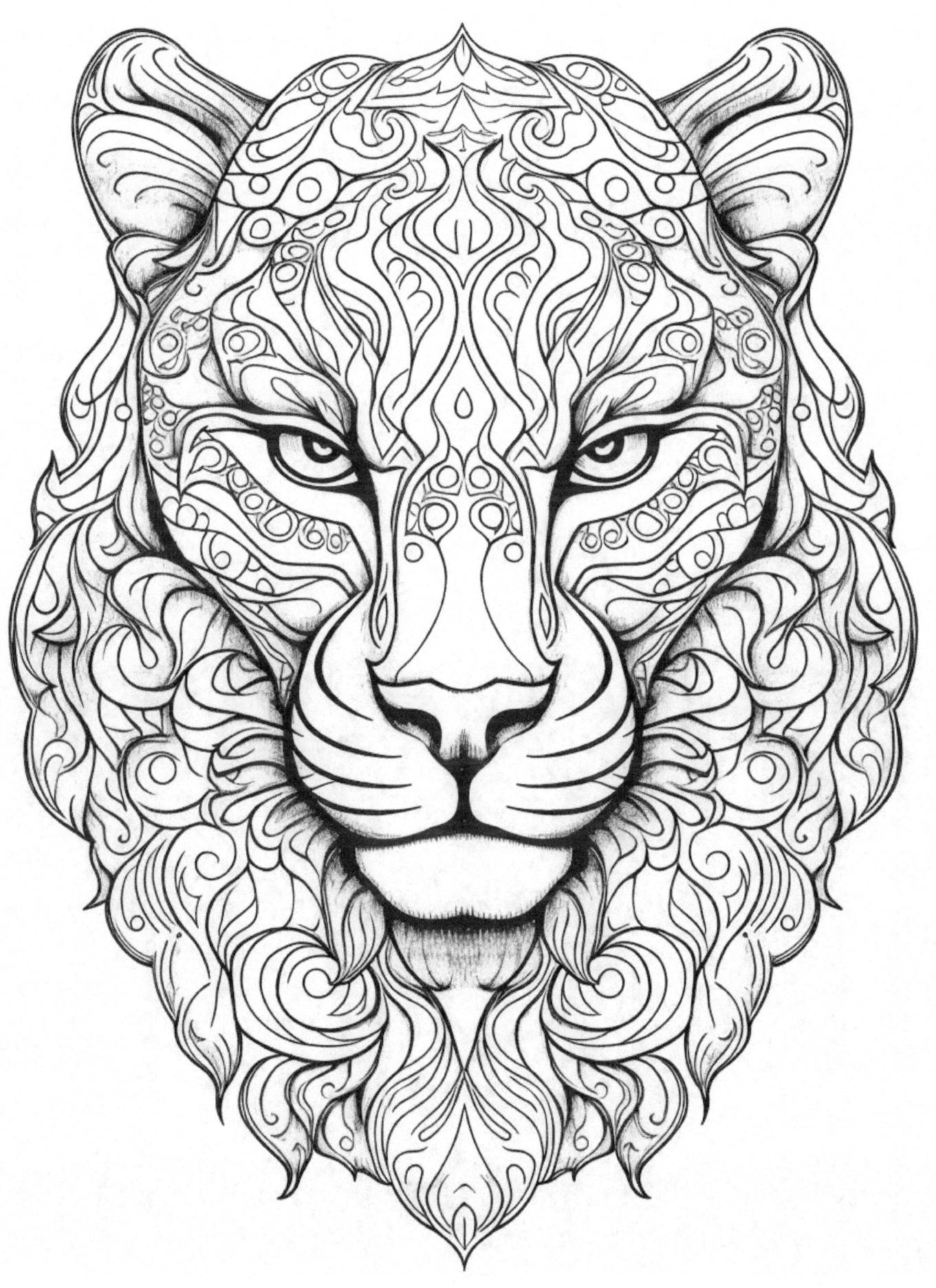

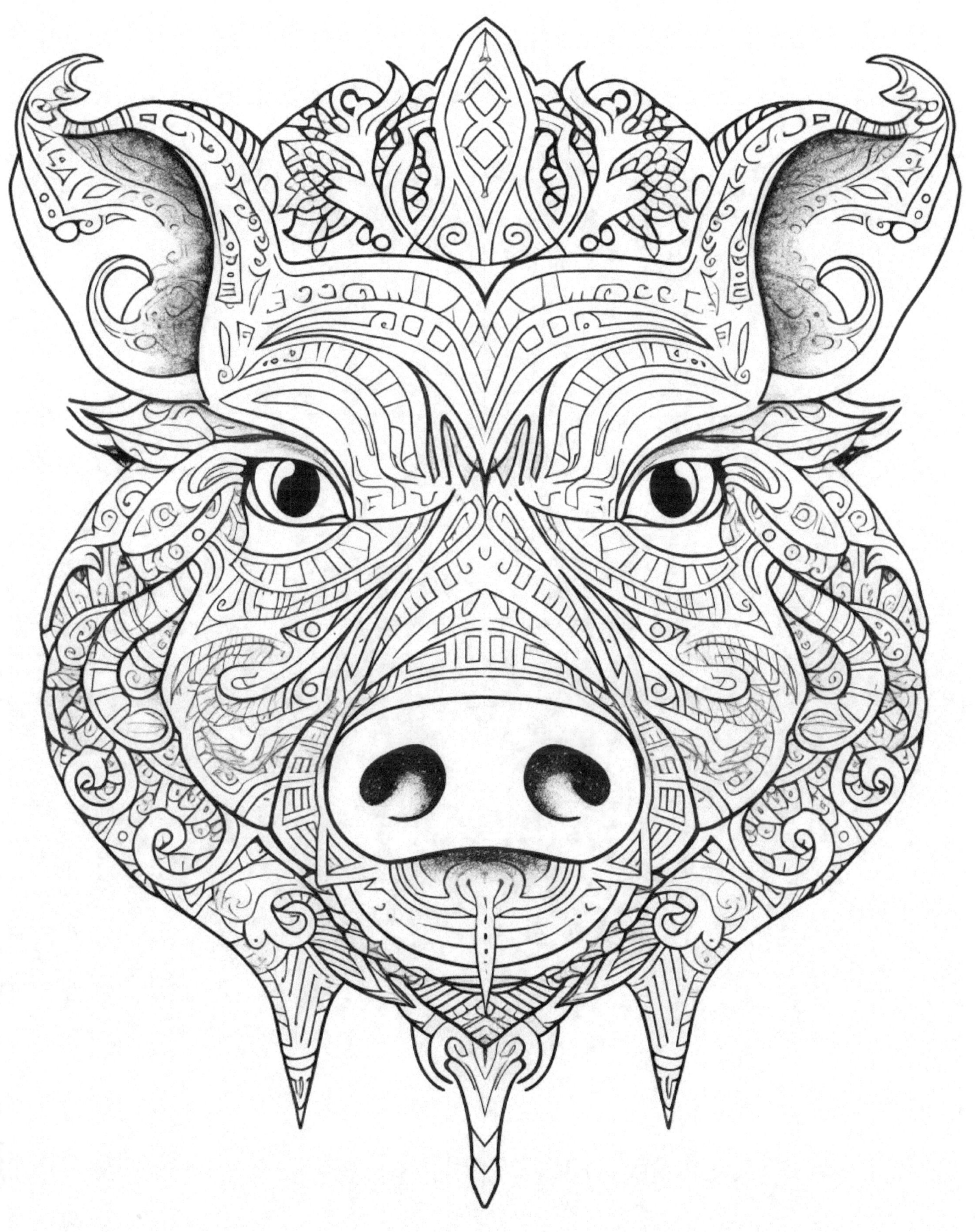

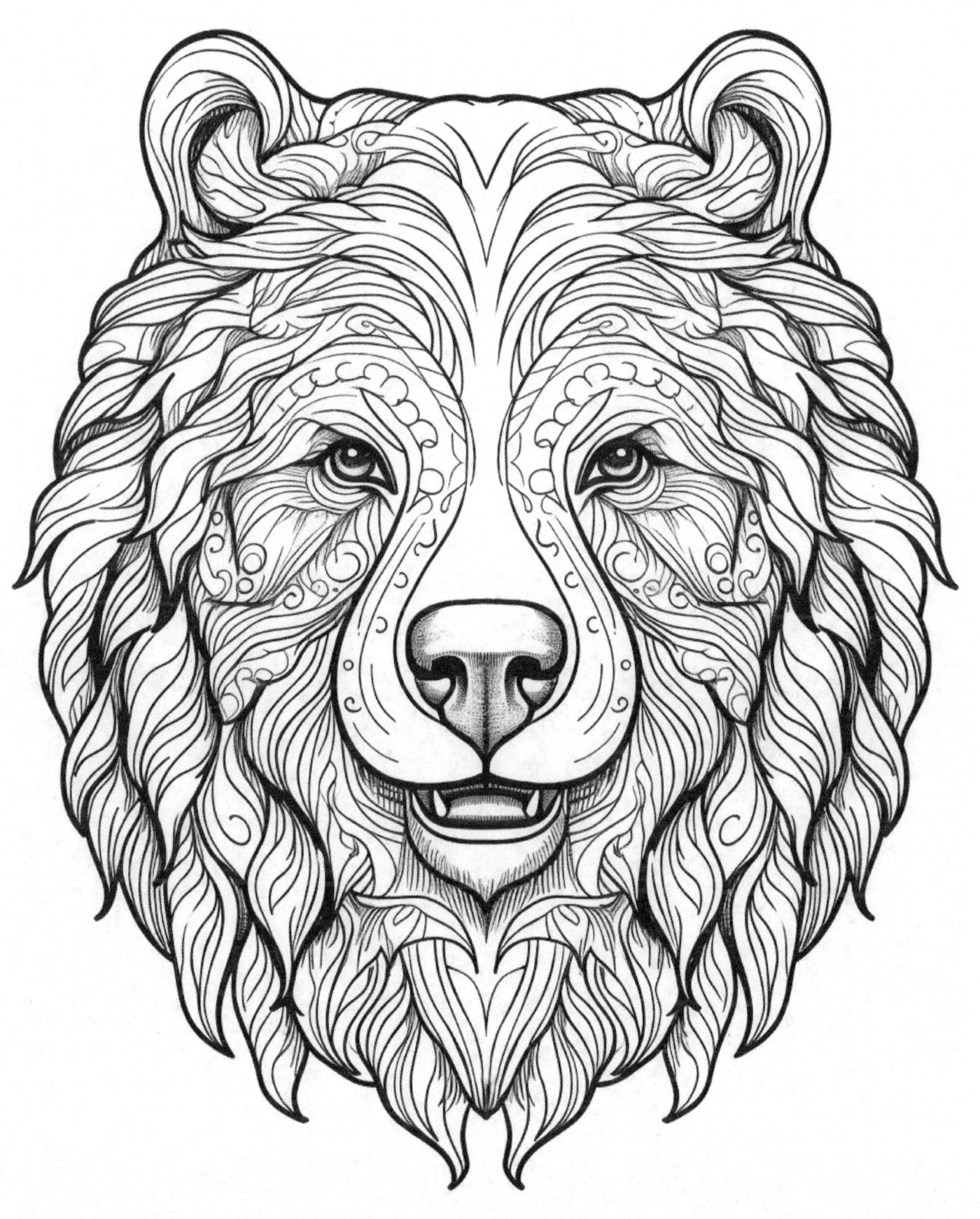

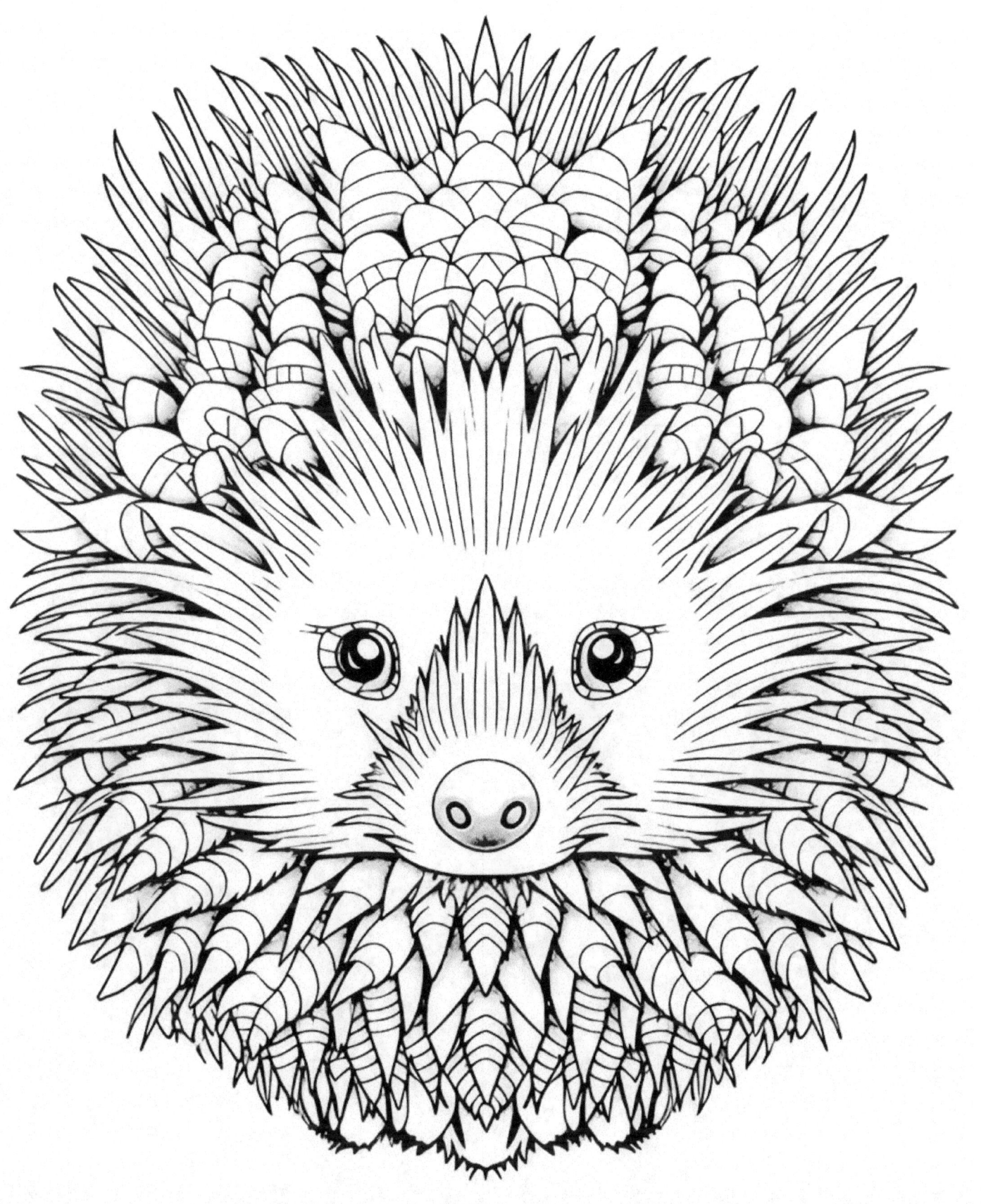

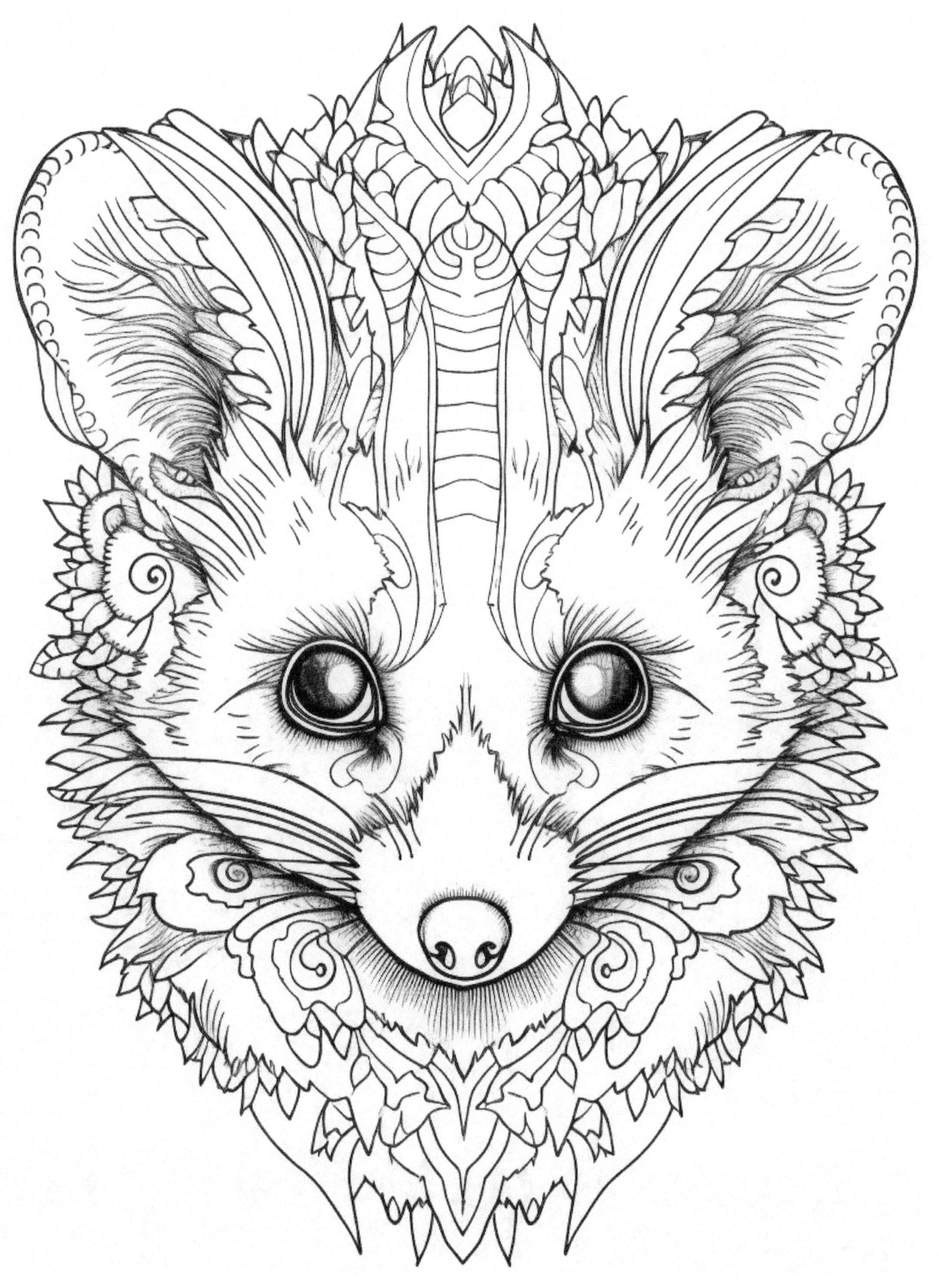

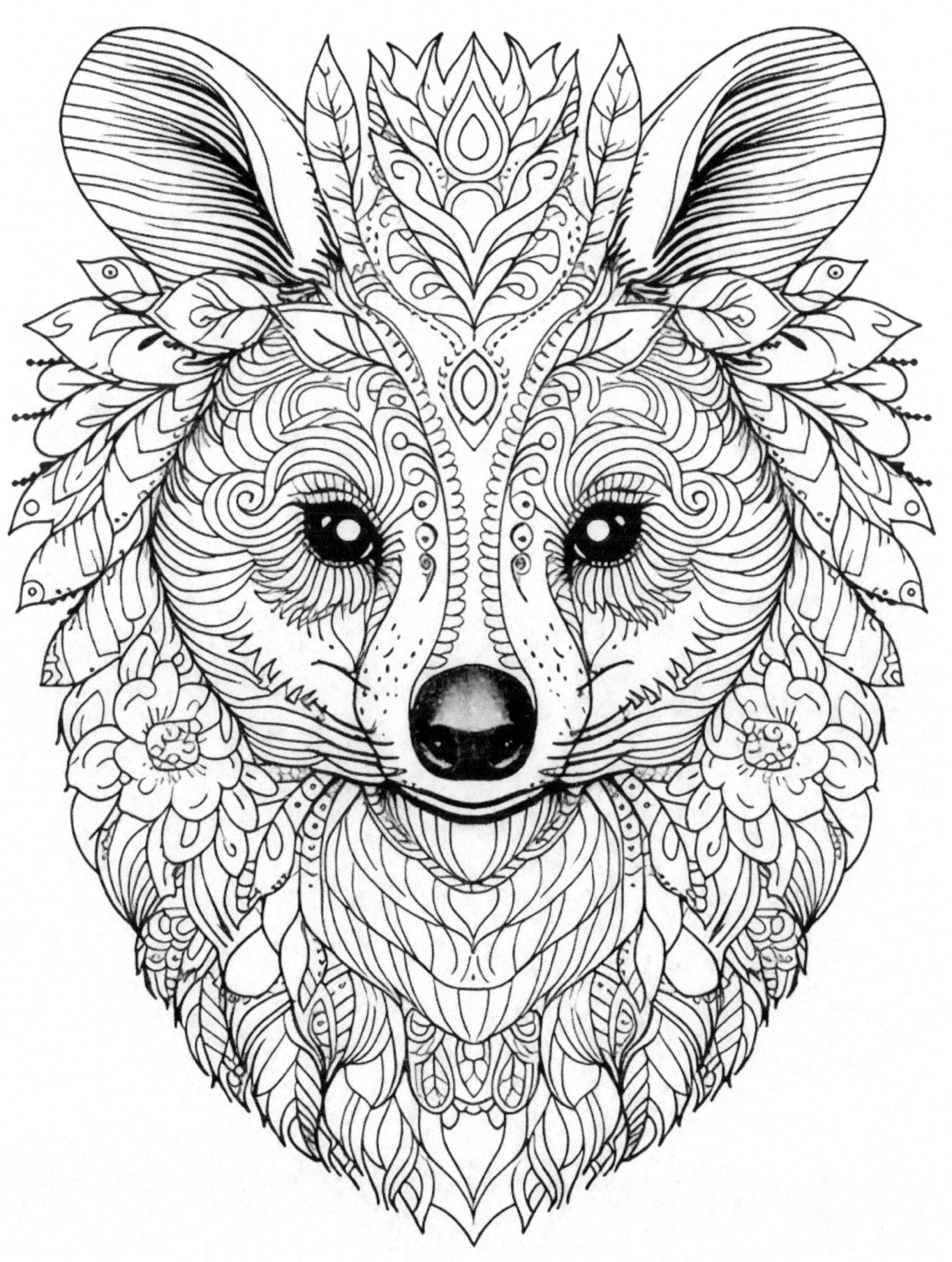

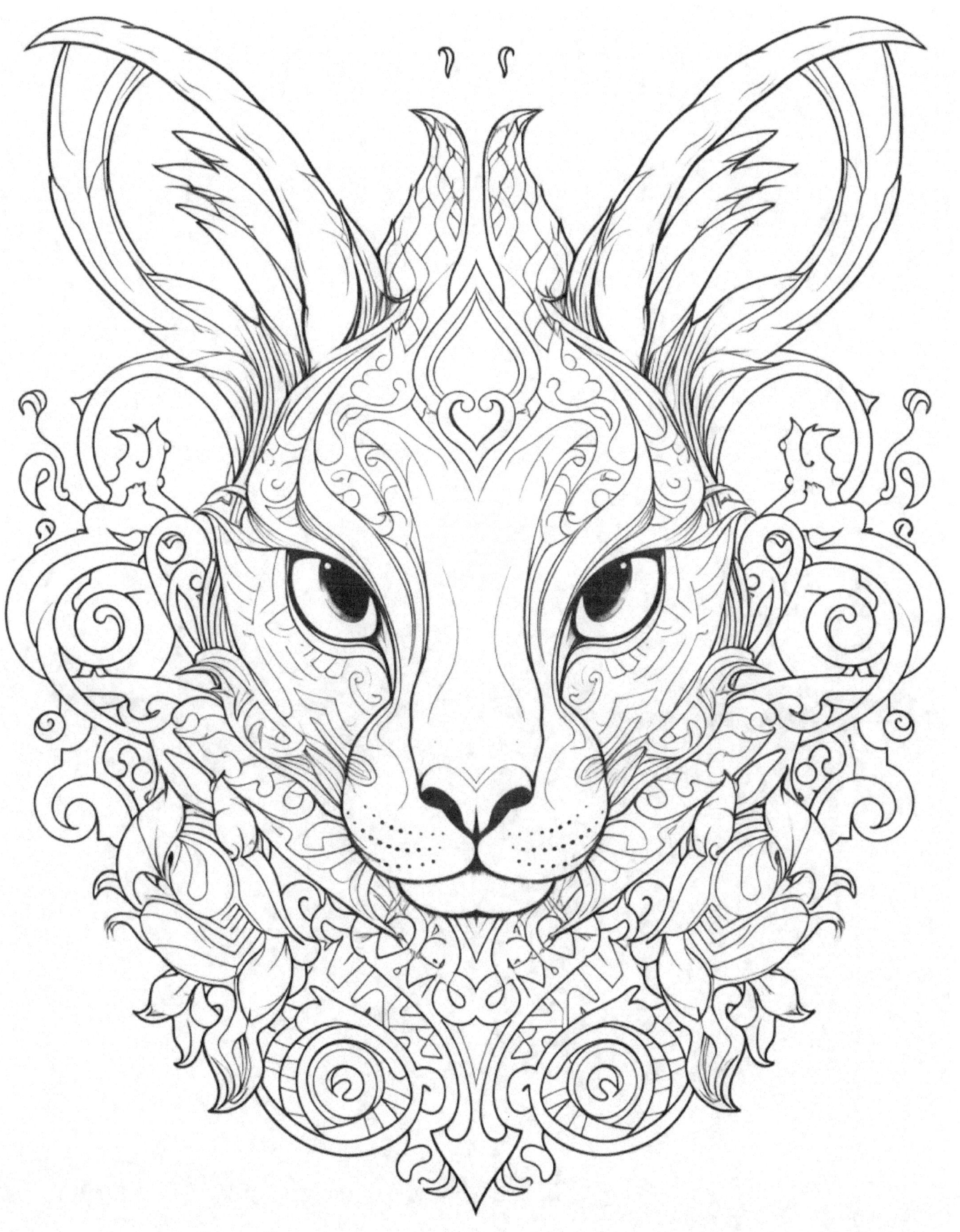

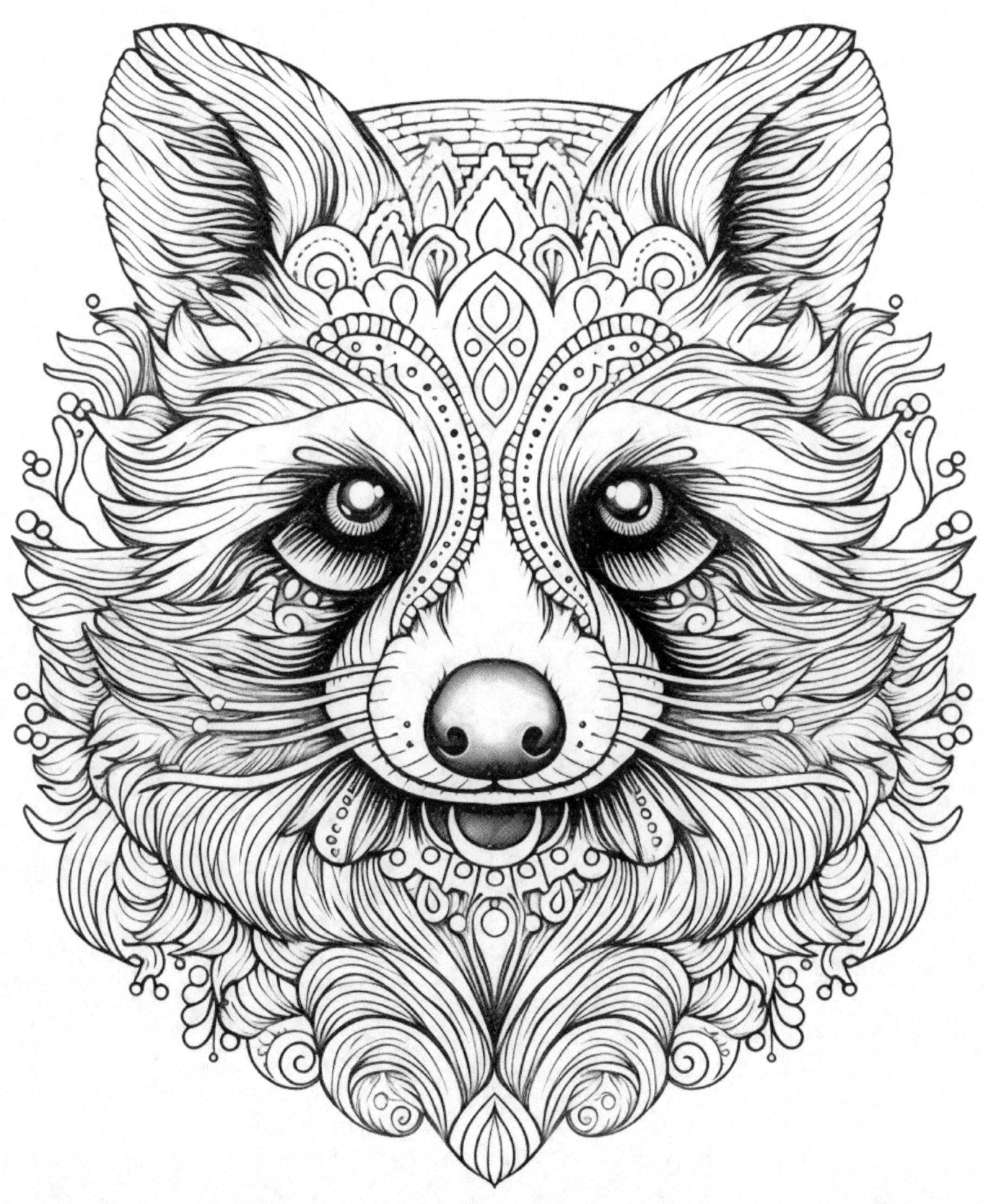

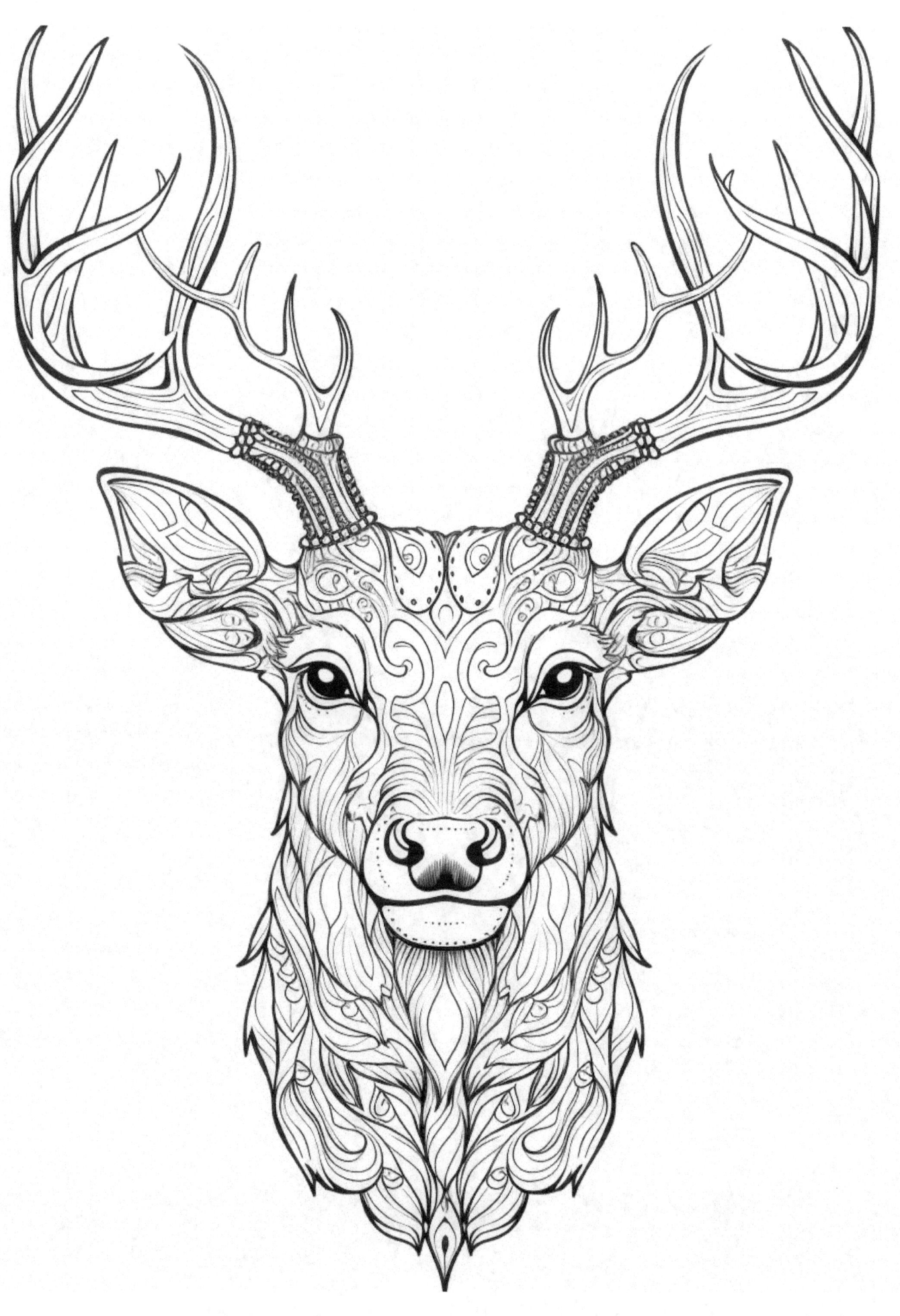

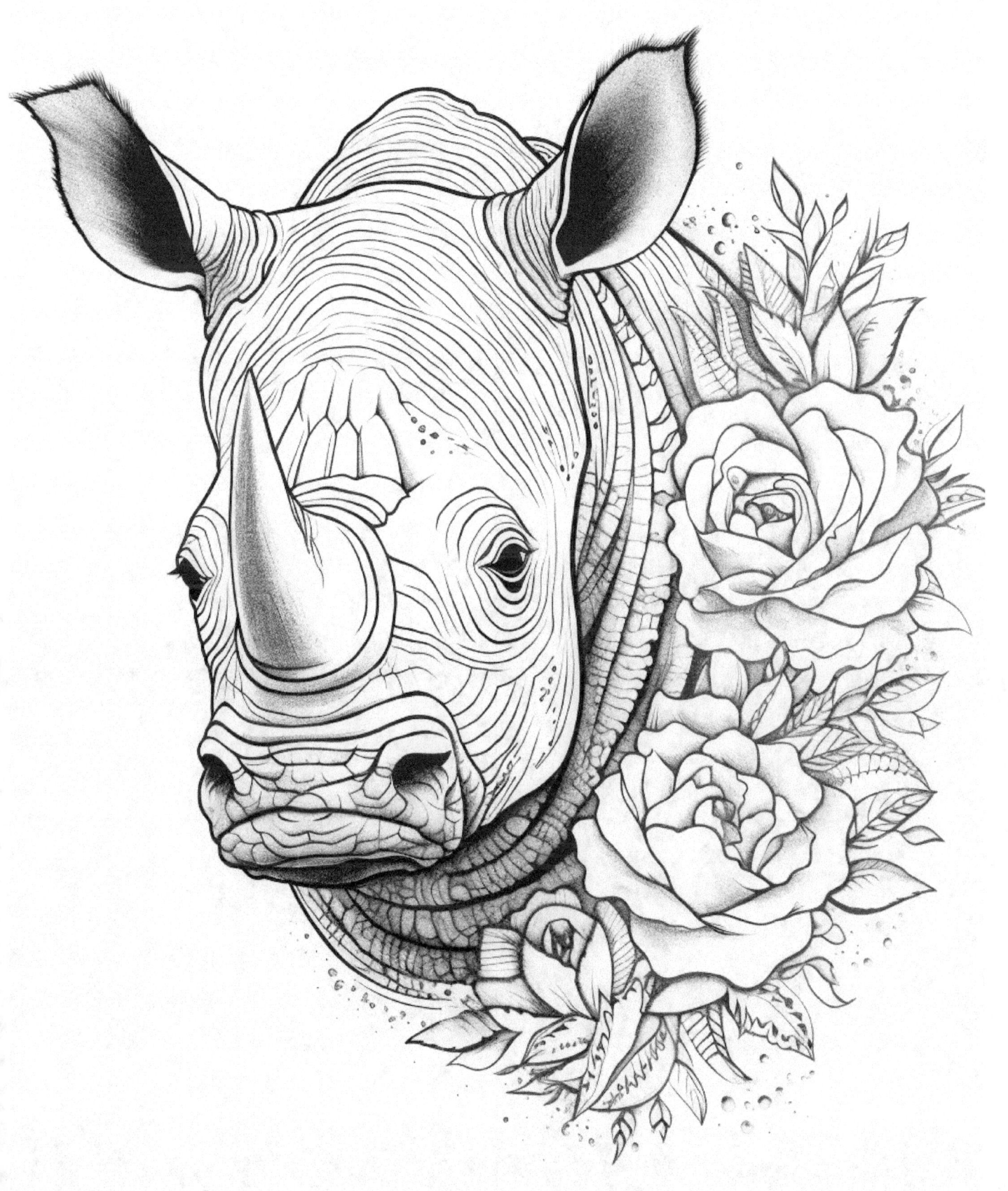

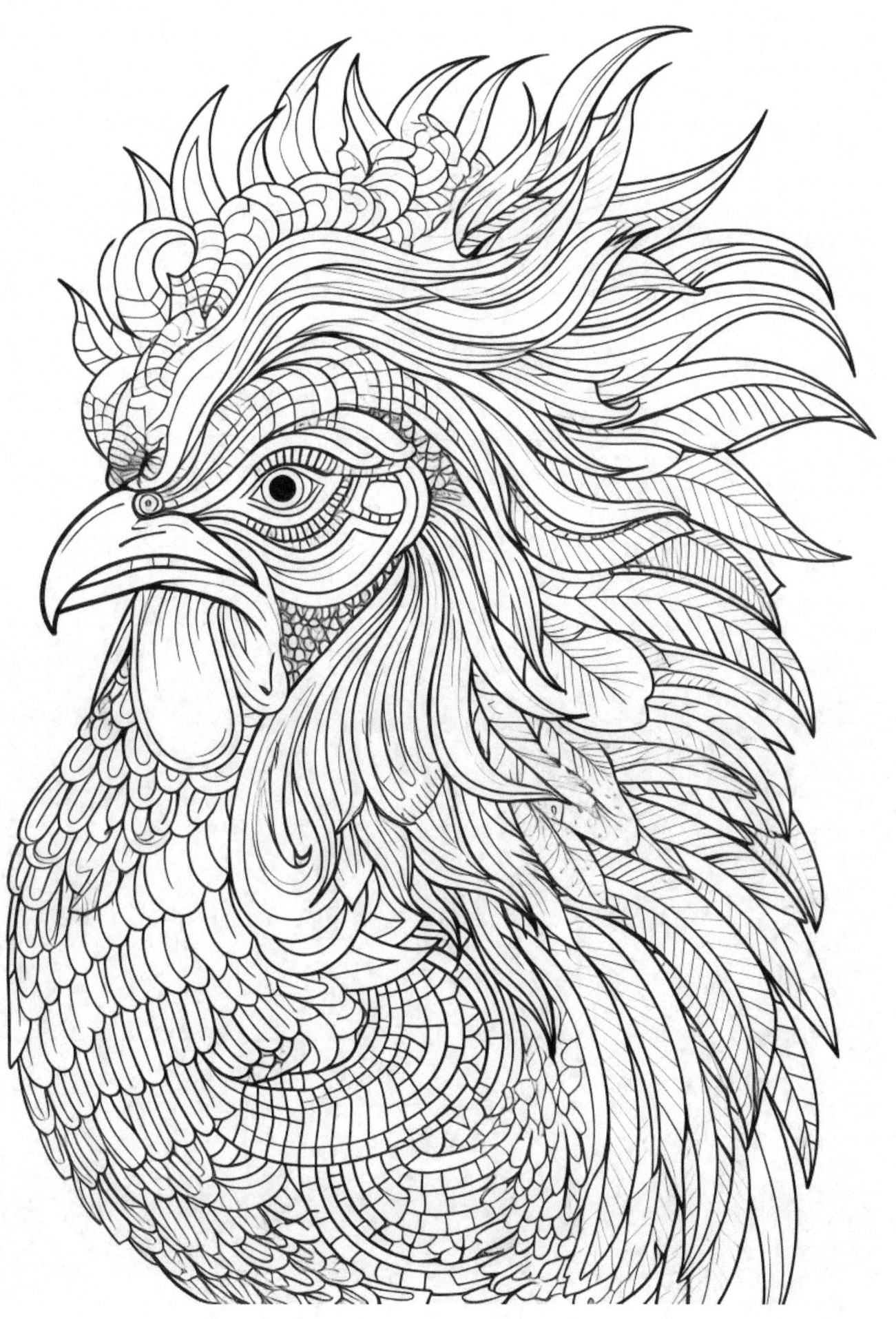

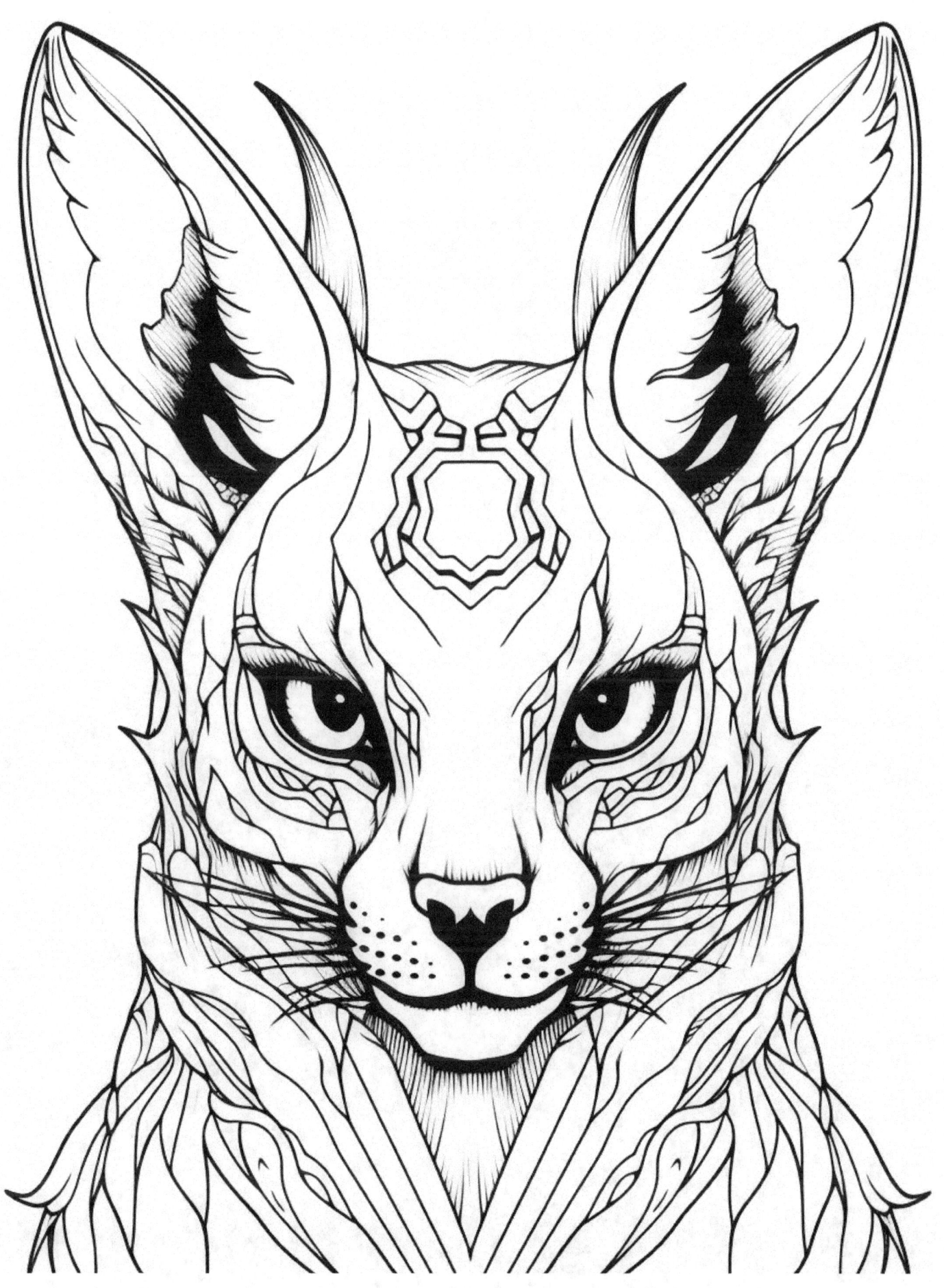

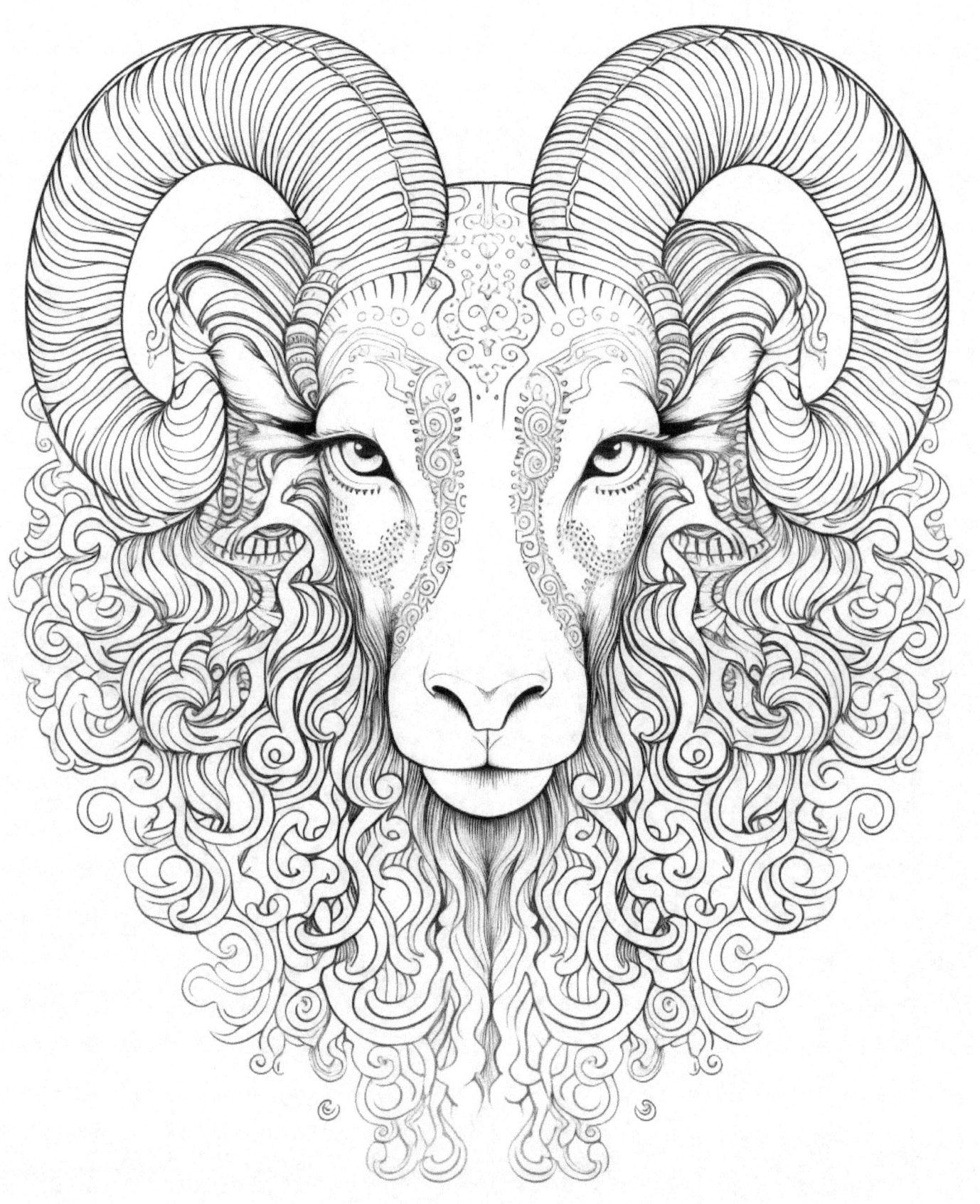

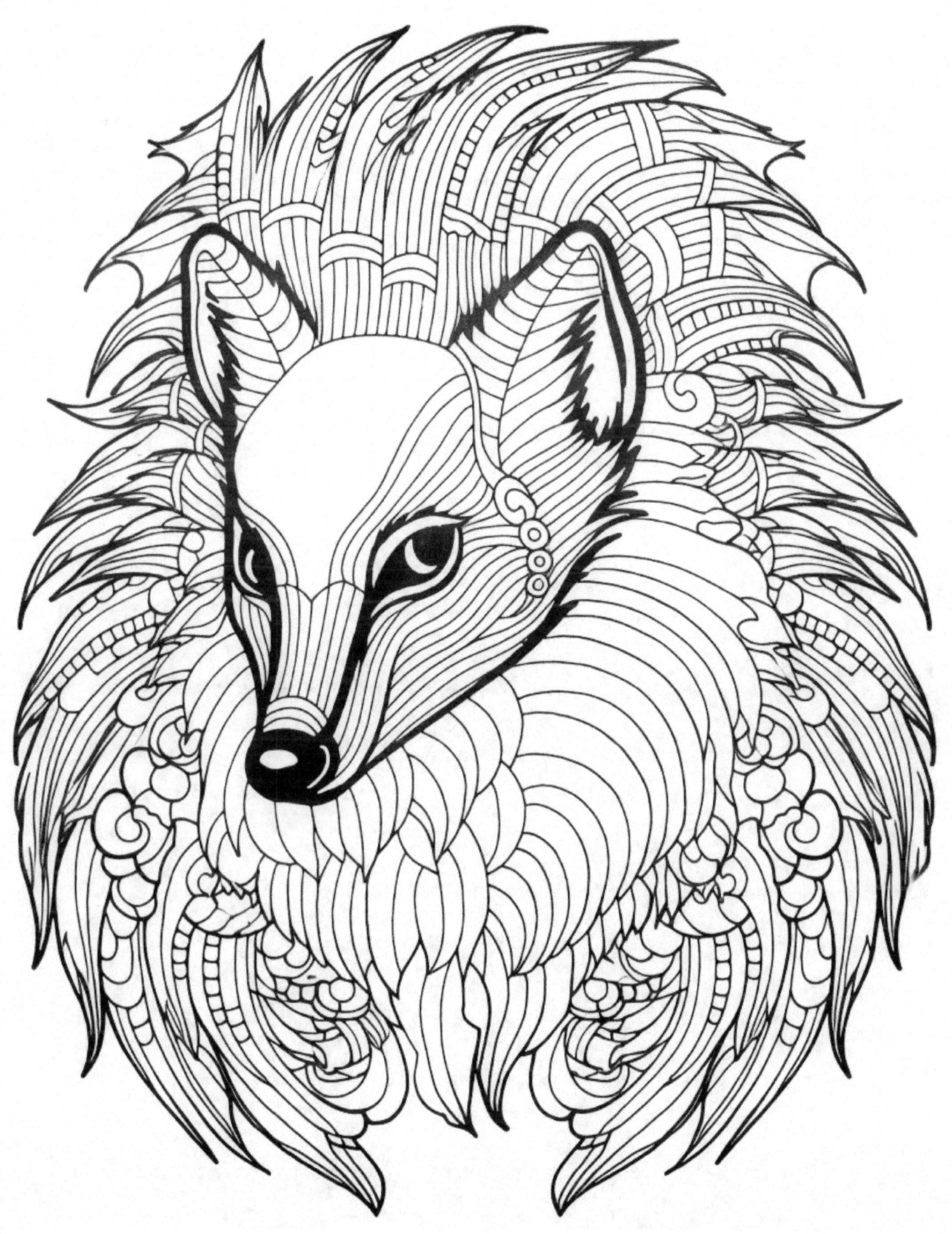

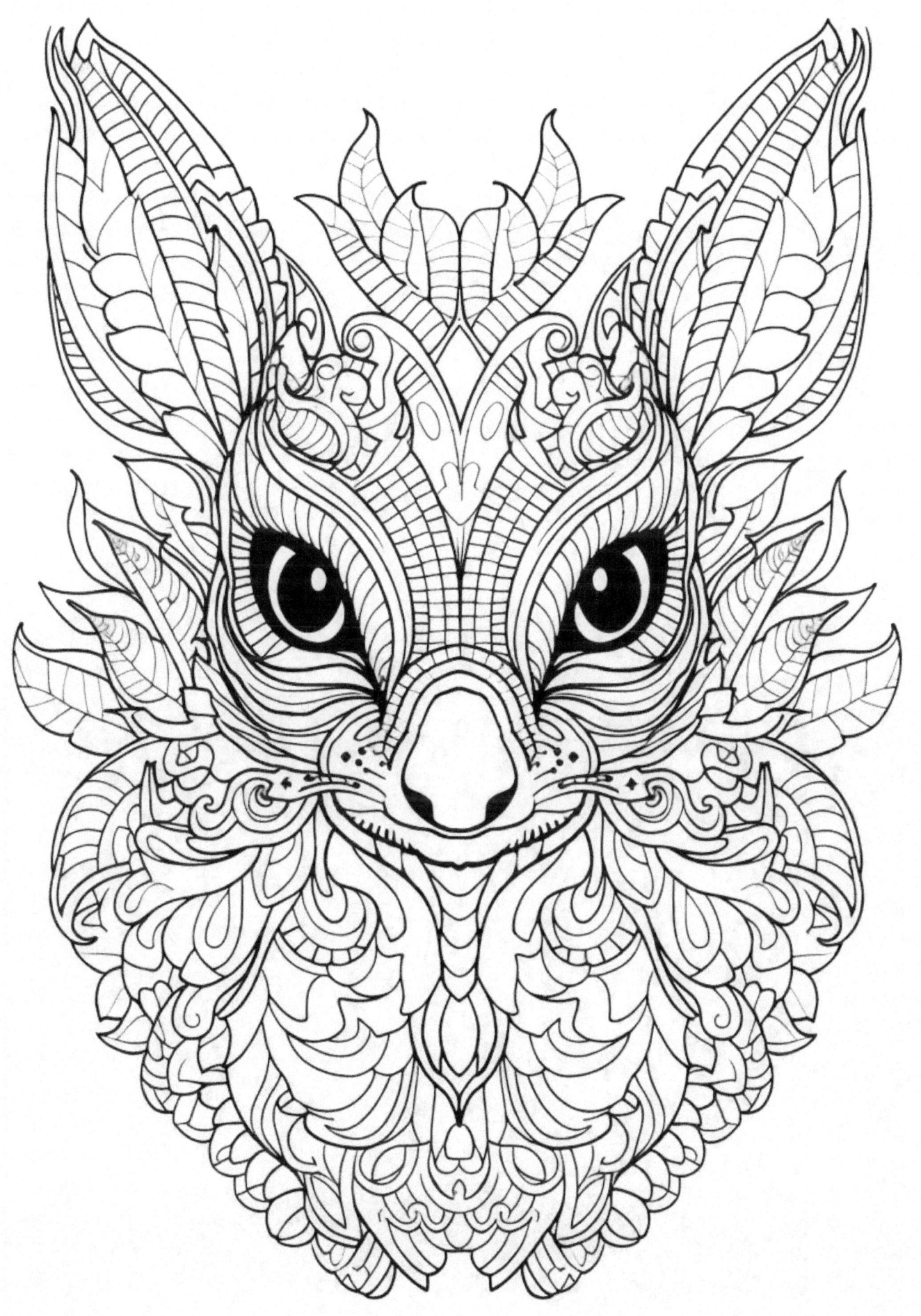

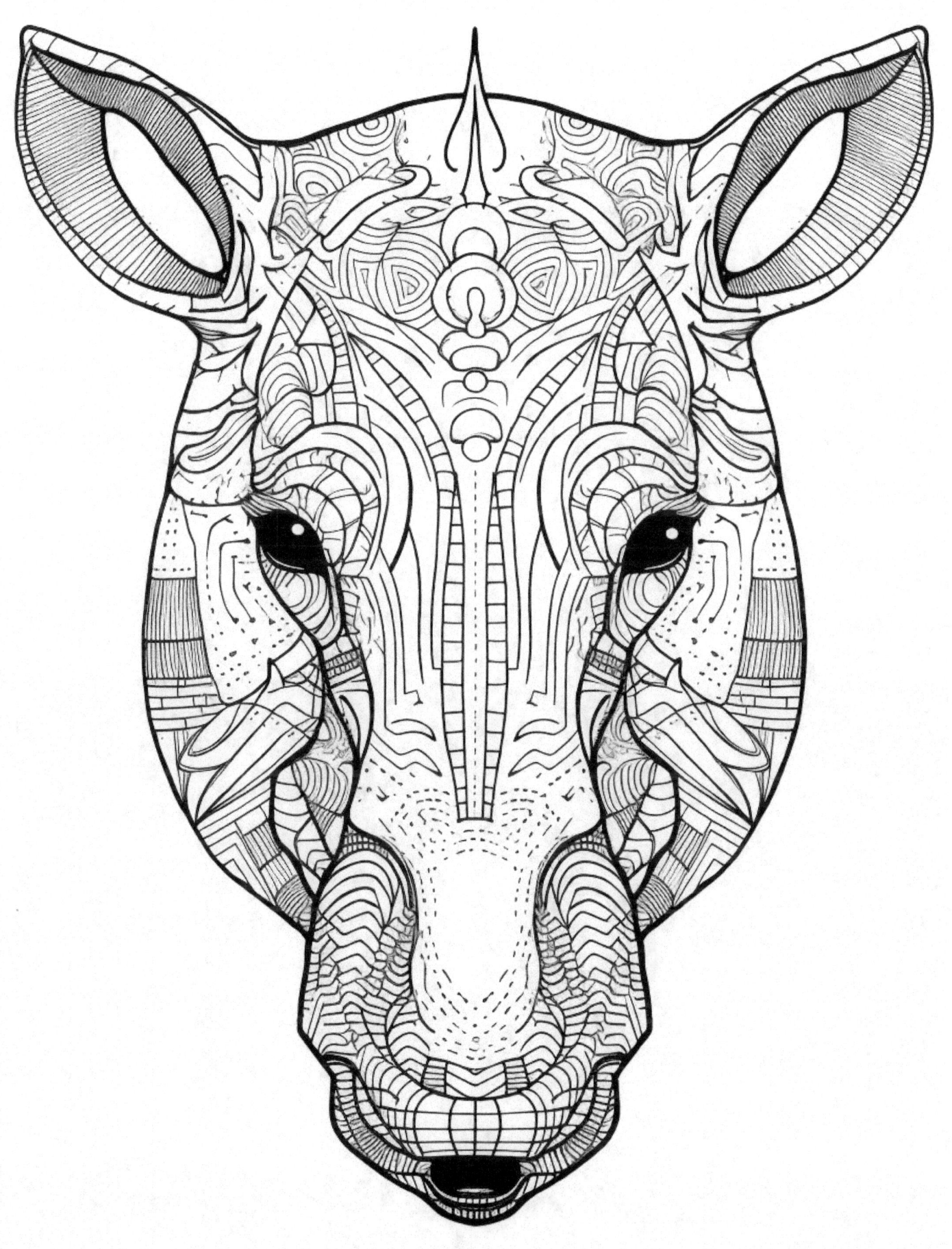

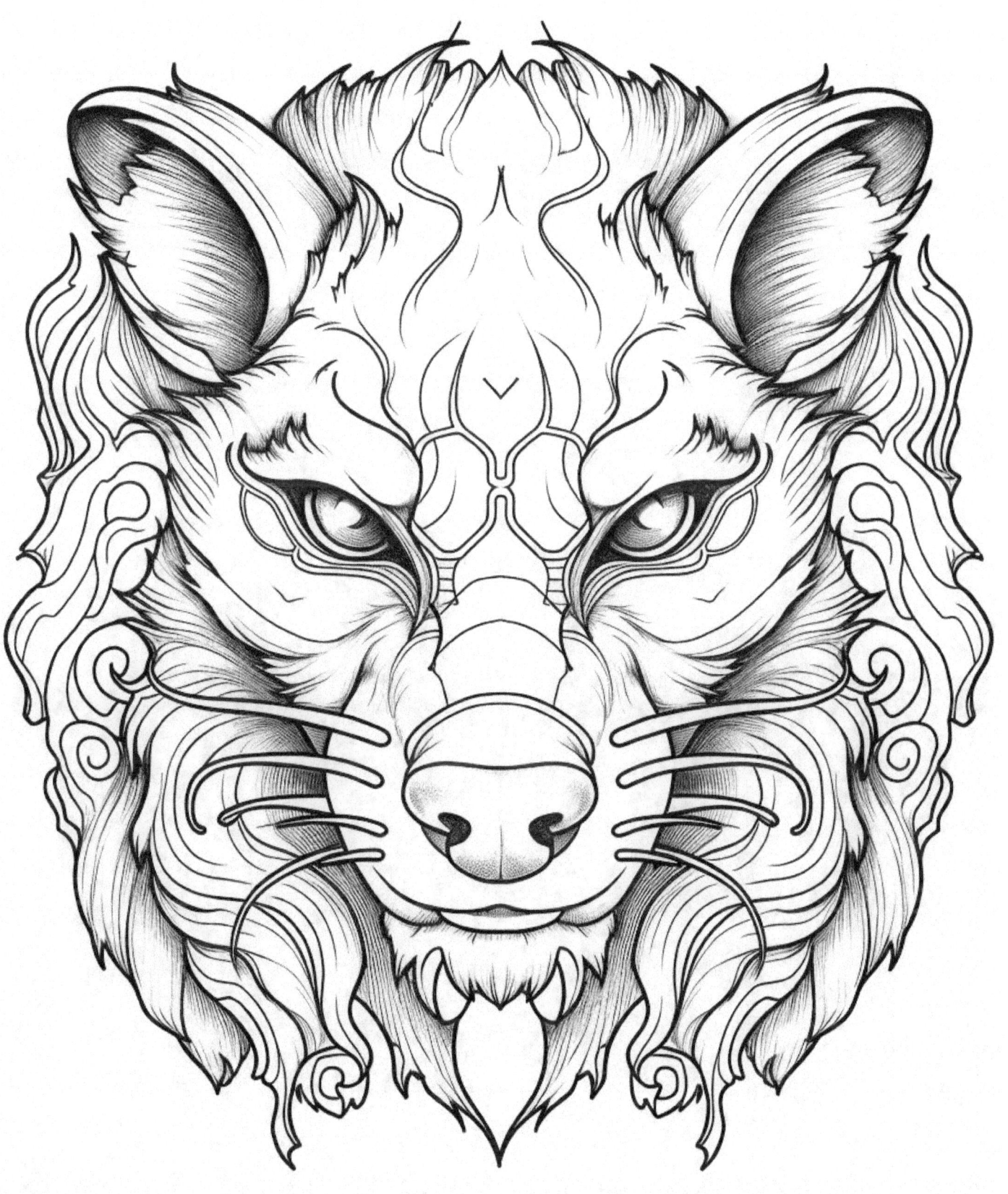

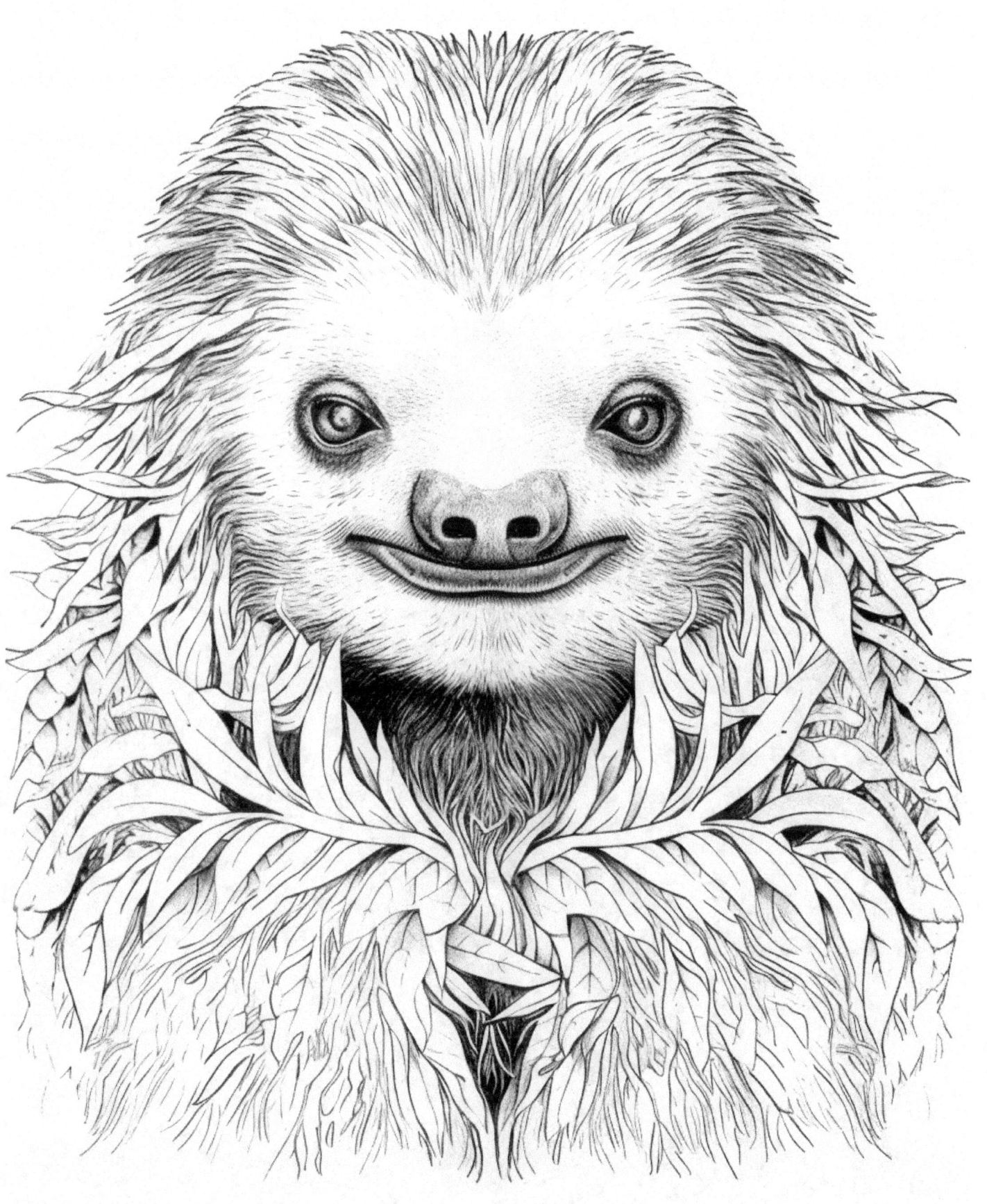

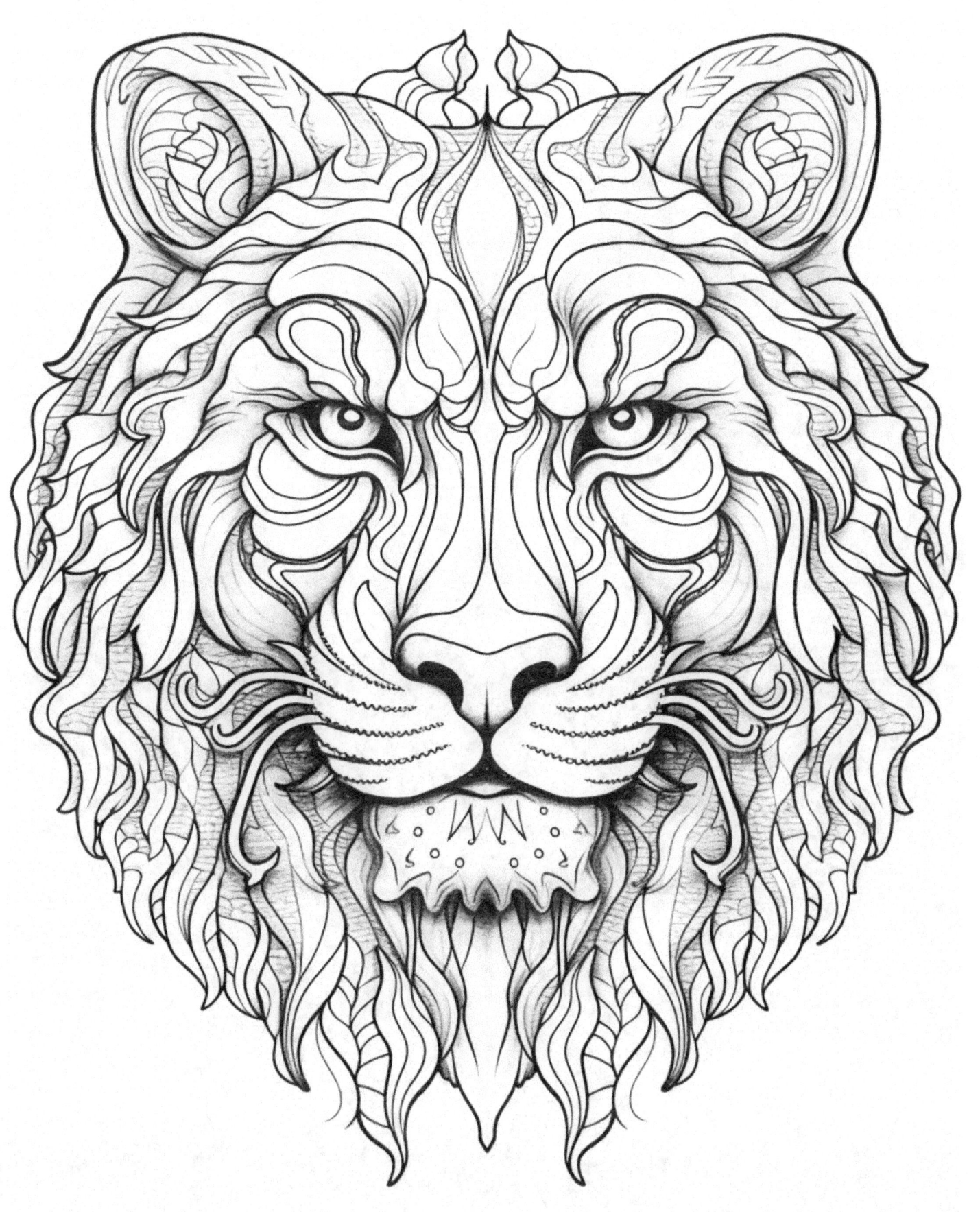

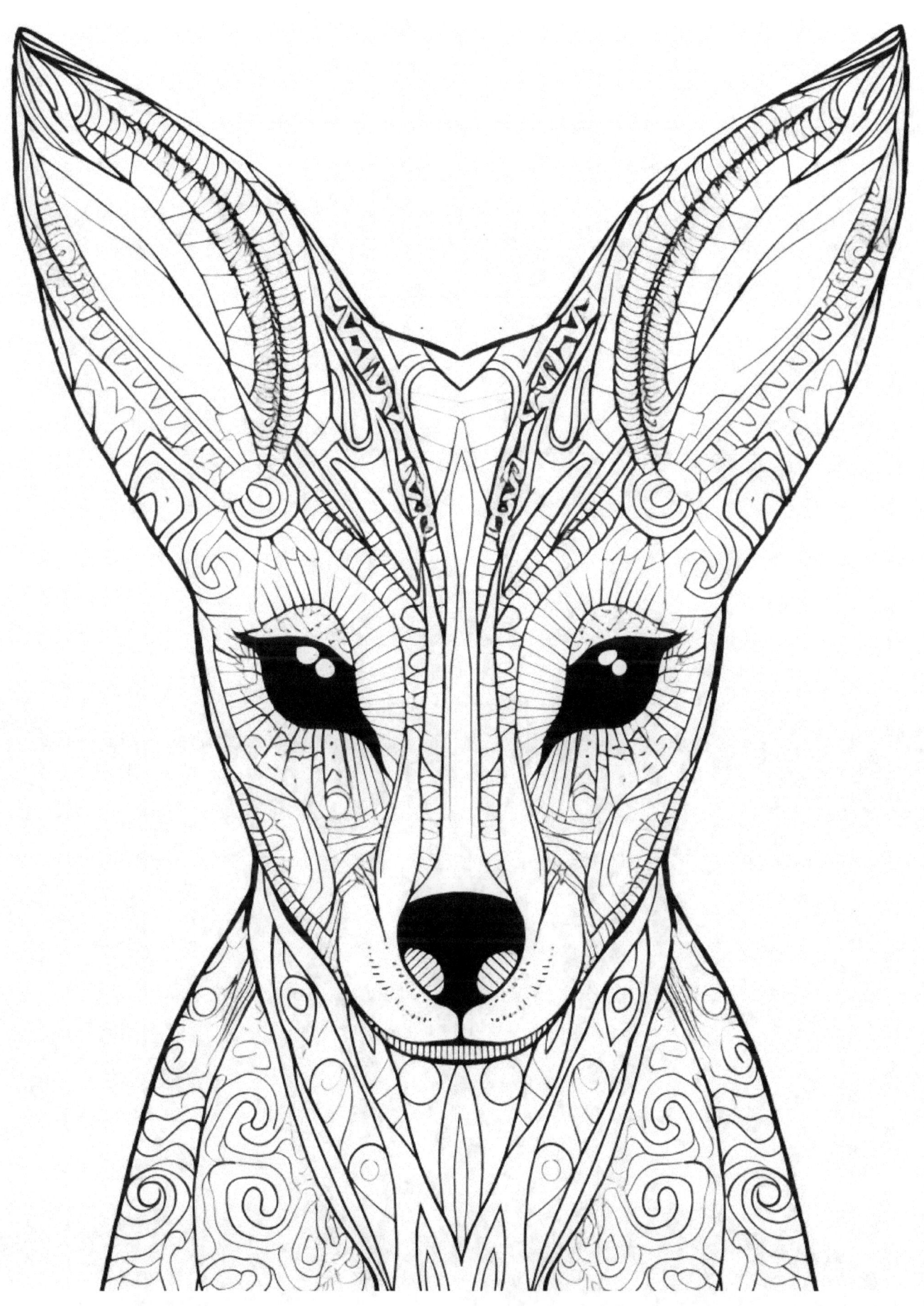

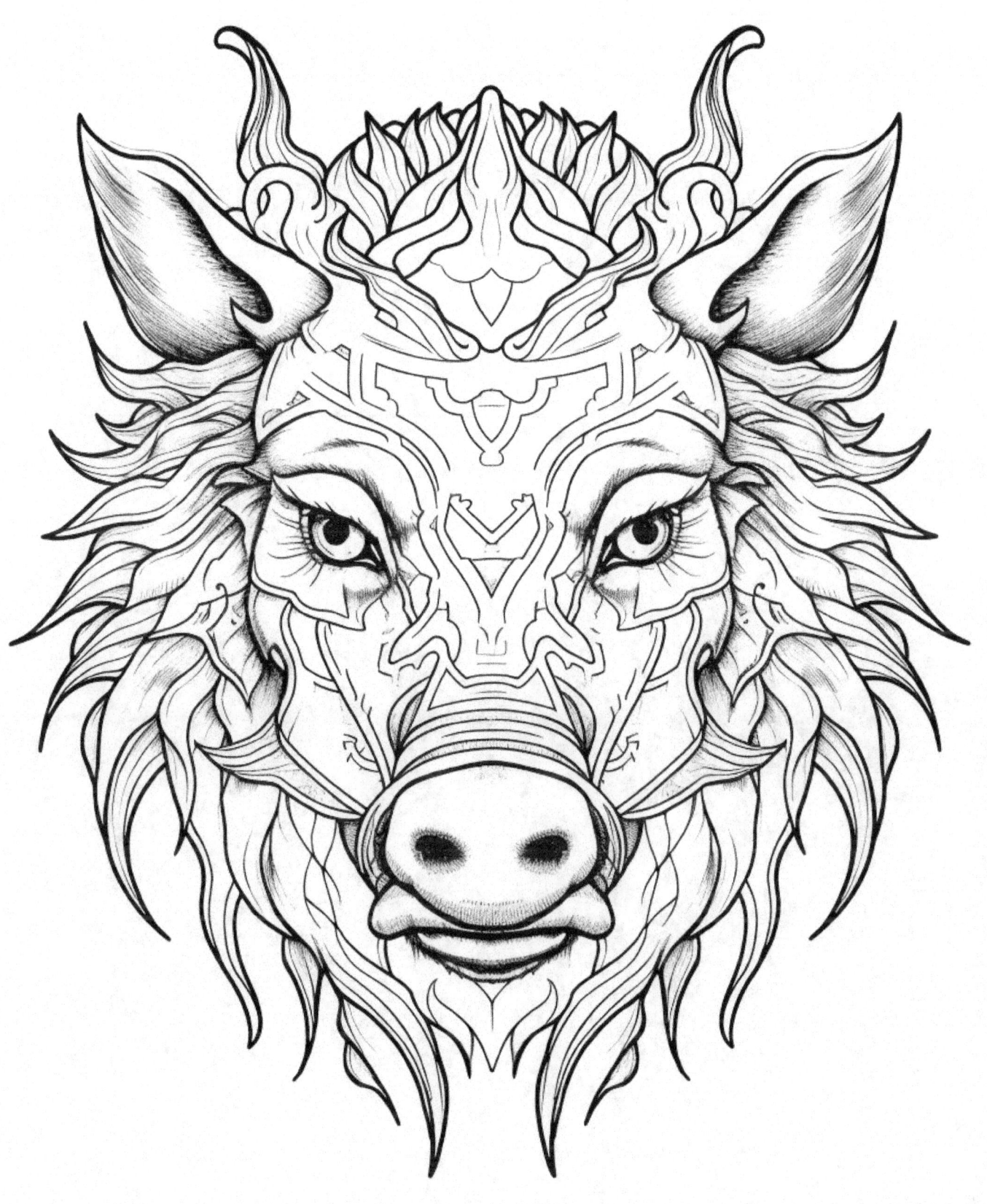

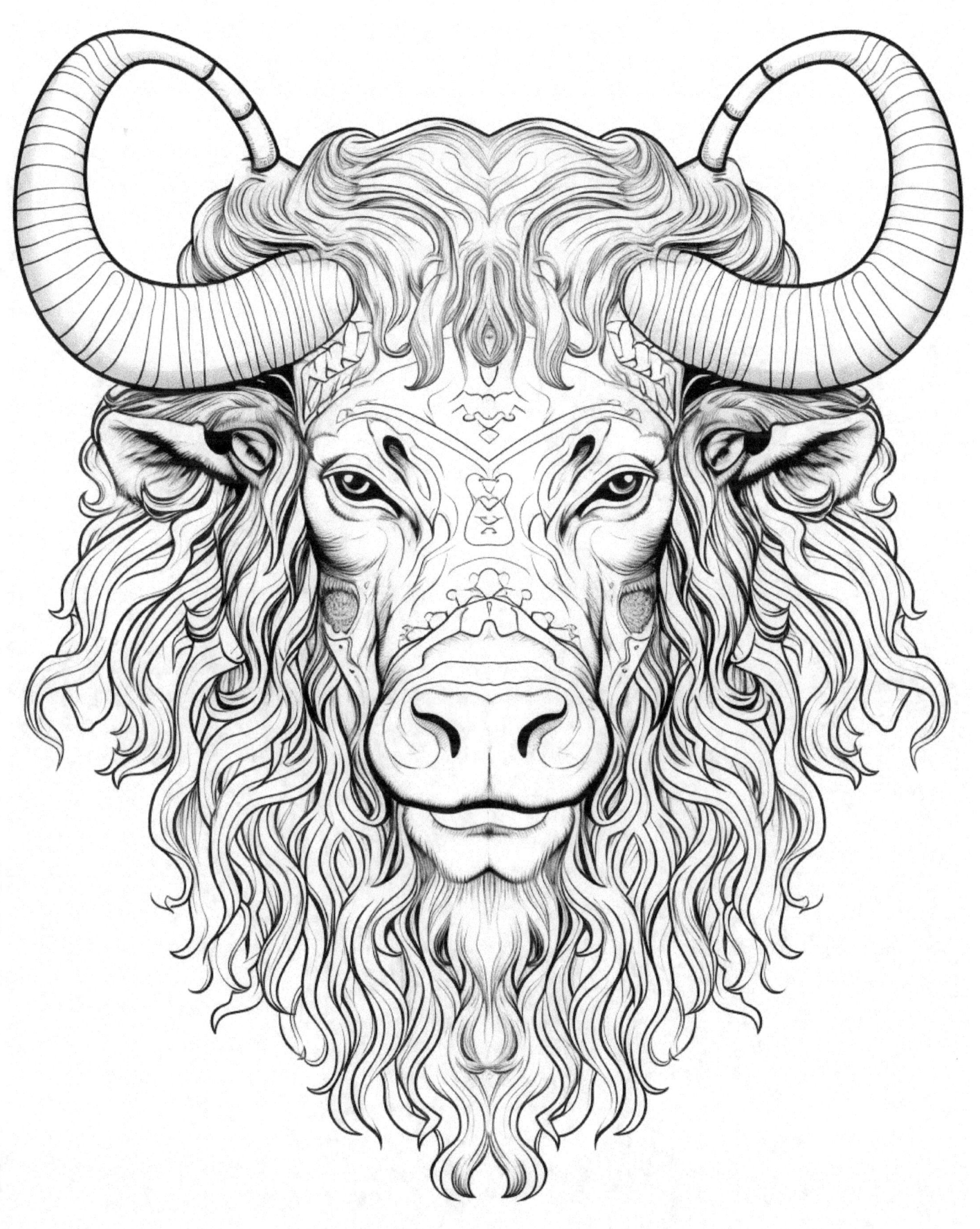

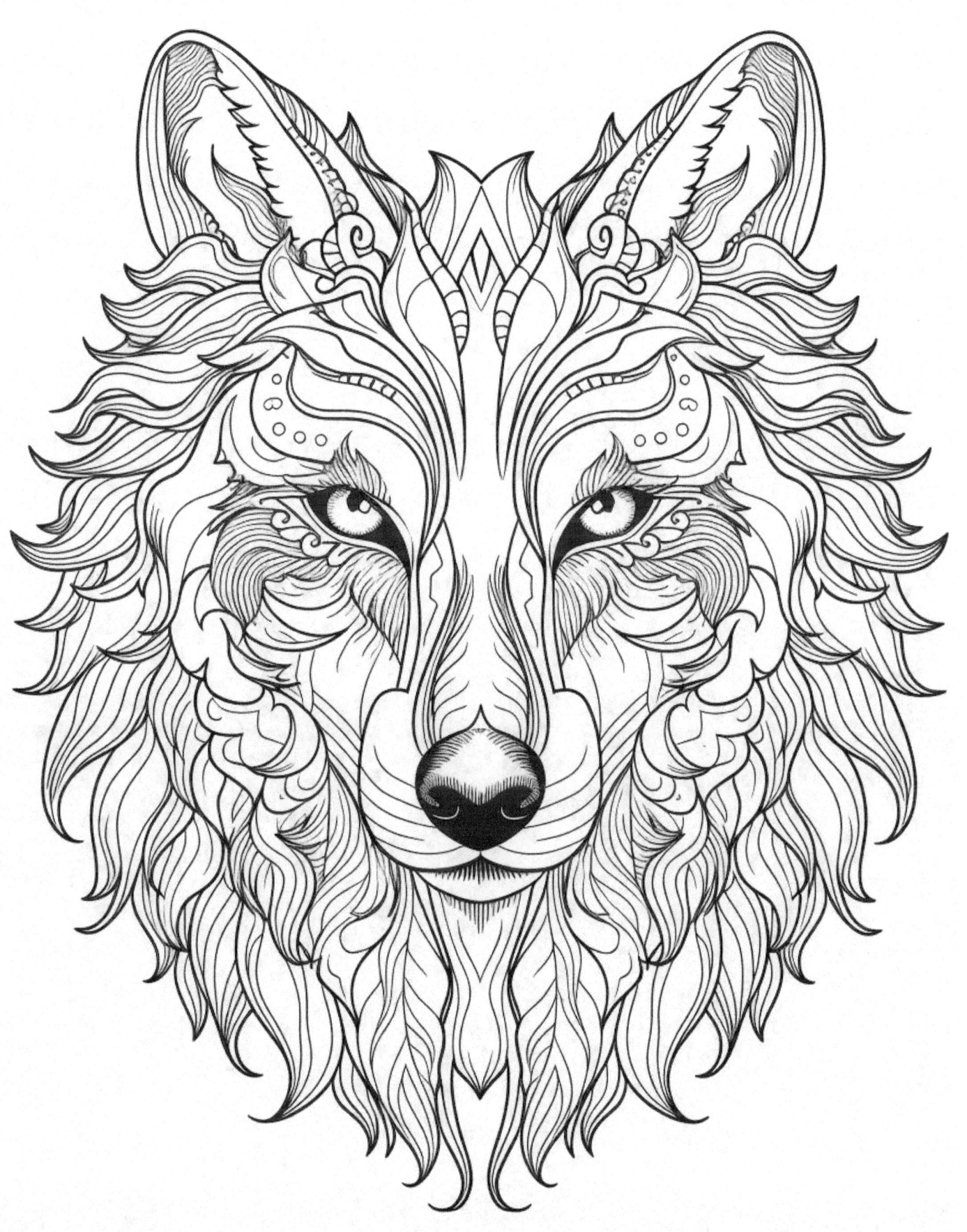

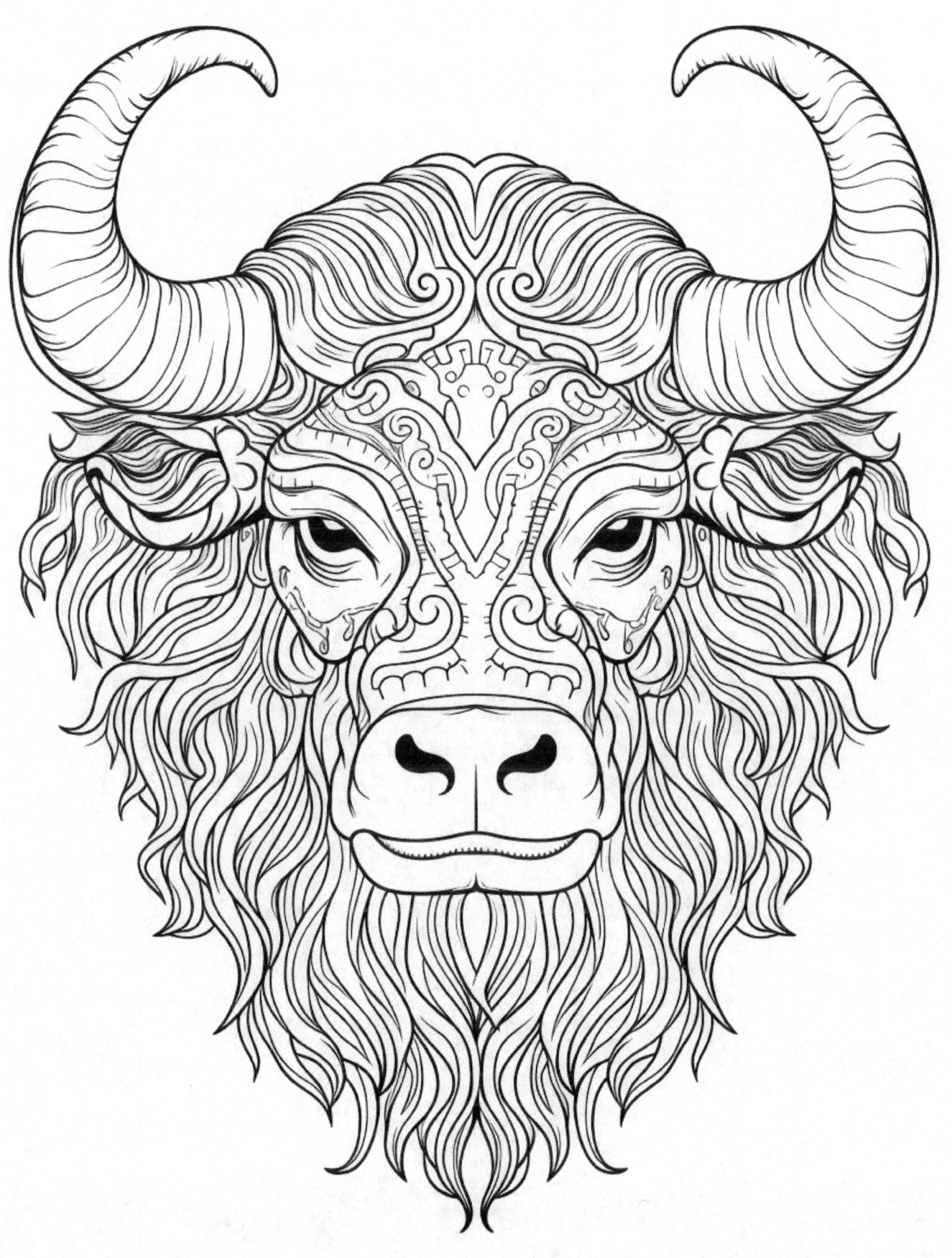

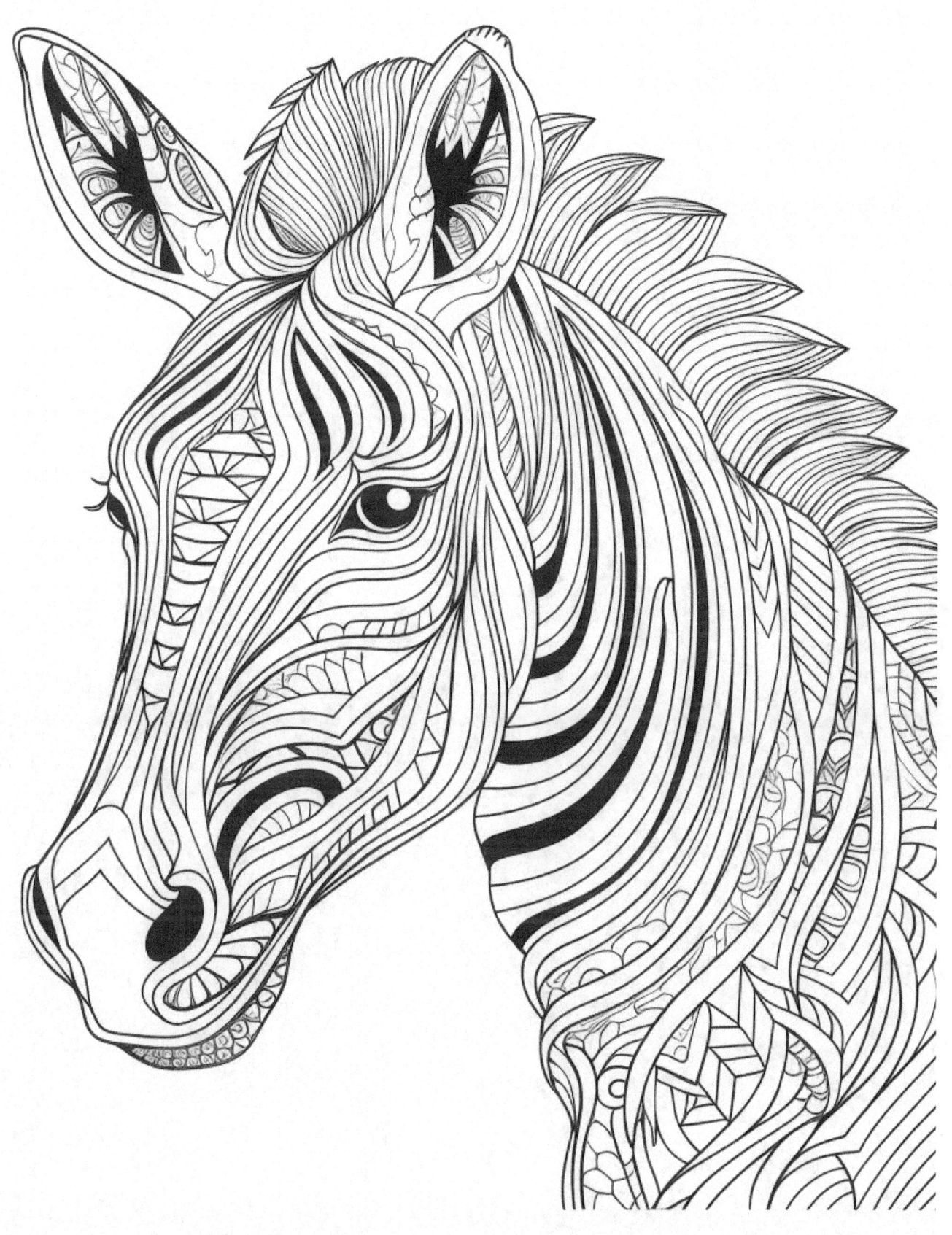